how Jewish Terrorist created the state of Israel

rajib christian

Published by rajib christian, 2024.

HOW JEWISH TERRORIST CREATED THE STATE OF ISRAEL

First edition. October 25, 2024.

ISBN: 979-8230094845

Written by rajib christian.

Table of Contents

"Every system has a story, and every story has its vulnerabilities."— Rajib Christian

About The Author

Rajib Christian is an investigative journalist, truth-seeker, and advocate for justice, known for tackling controversial and often overlooked issues. With a passion for exposing systemic abuses, Rajib Christian has spent years shedding light on stories that challenge the status quo and demand accountability.

Their latest book on Zionist terrorism is a deeply researched exposé, rooted in a fierce commitment to uncovering the hidden layers of violence, power, and oppression. It represents not just a scholarly effort but a moral pursuit—a dedication to giving voice to those silenced by historical and contemporary injustices.

Beyond their work on Zionist terrorism, Rajib Christian has written extensively on the victimization of Black women in the music industry, penning the groundbreaking article *"R. Kelly, Chris Brown, and Russell Simmons: A Portrait of the Music Industry and the Victimization of Black Women."* In this powerful piece, Rajib brings to the forefront the ongoing struggles of Black women, who often find themselves at the intersection of fame, abuse, and silence.

Their investigative work also includes in-depth reporting on police violence in America. In their article on Kim Potter, the white police officer who fatally shot Daunte Wright in Minnesota, Rajib Christian navigated the painful complexities of racial violence and the tragic consequences of systemic failures.

With a career marked by fearless storytelling, Rajib Christian continues to fight for truth, justice, and the rights of the oppressed—whether confronting international terrorism, industry exploitation, or state-sanctioned violence. Their writing is not just a reflection of the world's darkest realities but a call to action, pushing readers to confront uncomfortable truths and work towards meaningful change.

Unit	Leaders	Formed	Disbanded	Notable Actions/ Operations
Palestine Police Force (PPF)	- General Sir Arthur Grenfell Wauchope (High Commissioner 1931-1937)	1920	1948	- Suppression of the 1936–1939 Arab Revolt.
	- Sir Alan Cunningham (High Commissioner 1945–1948)			- Maintaining order during Jewish immigration waves (Aliyah Bet).
British Army in Palestine	- General Bernard Montgomery (Commander during WWII)	1917	1948	- Battles with Jewish insurgent groups (Irgun, Lehi).
	- General Sir Evelyn Barker (Commander of British forces, 1946–1947)			- Operations Agatha and Polly (anti-insurgency operations).
Royal Air Force (RAF)	- Air Vice Marshal Hugh Lloyd (Commander, 1945–1946)	1918	1948	- Aerial surveillance and support in maintaining order.
Transjordan Frontier Force	- Major General Frederick Peake (Founder)	1926	1948	- Policing border areas, assisting British

(TJFF)

forces during
Arab revolts.

French Military Units (French Mandate in Lebanon: 1920–1946)

Unit	Leaders	Formed	Disbanded	Notable Actions/ Operations
Armée du Levant (Army of the Levant)	- General Henri Gouraud (Commander, early years of the mandate) - General Georges Catroux (High Commissioner of Levant, 1941)	1920	1946	- Battle of Maysalun (1920) – Defeated Arab forces, secured mandate. - Suppression of Druze rebellion (1925–1927).
Troupes Spéciales du Levant (Special Troops)	- Colonel Edgar de Larminat (Commanded during early years)	1921	1946	- Served as local auxiliary forces alongside French military.
French Foreign Legion in the Levant	- General Charles de Gaulle (Led Free French Forces during WWII)	1920	1946	- Defended Vichy-controlled Lebanon, later supported Free French.

Additional Notes:

- The **Palestine Police Force (PPF)** became infamous for its role in suppressing uprisings by both Arabs and Jewish insurgent groups throughout the mandate.

- The **Transjordan Frontier Force (TJFF)** was mainly responsible for patrolling and securing the borders of British-controlled Palestine and Transjordan.

- The **British Army** and **RAF** faced extensive conflict from both Jewish paramilitary groups and Arab nationalists, leading to several large-scale military operations.

- The **Armée du Levant** and **Troupes Spéciales** played crucial roles in both suppressing local uprisings and maintaining French control over the Levant.

- **France** officially ended its mandate over Lebanon in 1946, after increasing pressure from Lebanese nationalists and the global decolonization movement.

The Demographics of Palestine 1922
the **demographic breakdown of Palestine from the 1922 Census,** which was conducted under the British Mandate:

Group	Population	Percentage (%)
Total Population	757,182	100%
Muslims	590,890	78.0%
Jews	83,794	11.1%
Christians	73,024	9.6%
Others	9,474	1.3%

Breakdown by Religion and Ethnicity:

● **Muslims**: Predominantly Sunni Muslims, including some Bedouins.

● **Jews**: Mostly concentrated in urban areas such as Jerusalem, Jaffa, and Haifa.

● **Christians**: Primarily Orthodox Christians, with smaller communities of Catholics, Protestants, and other denominations.

● **Others**: Included small populations of Druze, Baha'i, and Samaritans.

This census provides an essential snapshot of the population distribution in Palestine during the early stages of the British Mandate period.

Exploring the Role of Zionist Terrorism in the Establishment of Israel

Zionist terrorism played a controversial and impact role during the final years of British rule in Palestine, significantly shaping the events that led to Israel's founding. Facing restrictions on Jewish immigration and land purchases, militant groups like the Irgun, Lehi (also known as the Stern Gang), and factions within the Haganah resorted to violence as a means of undermining British control and accelerating the end of the British Mandate.

Notable incidents such as the 1946 bombing of the King David Hotel and the 1948 Deir Yassin massacre were designed to shock, destabilize, and disrupt British governance and the Arab population in Palestine. Although these brutal actions were widely condemned, they effectively drew global attention to the Zionist cause, increasing pressure on Britain to exit Palestine.

Following the British withdrawal and the UN partition plan, Israel declared its independence in May 1948. Despite ongoing moral and ethical debates, these acts of terrorism undeniably reshaped the political landscape, ultimately contributing to the creation of the State of Israel.

The recent escalation of the Israeli-Palestinian conflict—such as the October 7, 2023, Hamas attack that resulted in over 1,200 Israeli deaths and thousands of injuries—highlights the enduring complexity of this conflict. This attack by Hamas, framed as a response to Israel's continued occupation and blockade of Gaza, mirrors a long history of retaliatory violence. To understand these contemporary events, it is essential to examine the historical roots of this conflict, particularly the British Mandate period (1920-1948) and the rise of Zionist militancy.

The British Mandate over Palestine marked a pivotal period of tension and transformation in the region. The Zionist movement's vision for a Jewish homeland increasingly clashed with the nationalist aspirations of the indigenous Arab population. This struggle gave rise to militant Zionist organizations whose acts of violence and armed resistance against both British rule and Arab communities profoundly shaped the geopolitical dynamics of the region.

Groups like the Irgun and Lehi used bombings, assassinations, and guerrilla warfare to destabilize British authority and advance their goal of establishing a Jewish state. The Haganah, initially formed as a defensive organization, evolved into a more offensive force, eventually becoming the foundation for the Israel Defense Forces (IDF) in 1948. While these groups played a crucial role in the creation of Israel, their actions also laid the groundwork for future conflict with Palestinian Arabs.

The legacy of early Zionist militancy continues to shape modern Israeli and Palestinian societies. It has influenced narratives, policies, and attitudes that perpetuate cycles of violence, making it crucial to understand these historical origins when analyzing today's Israeli-Palestinian conflict.

Assassinations as a retaliatory measure were a long-standing tactic within Zionist militias, predating the establishment of Israel. Early Zionist nationalists also used violence against international organizations, including the United Nations, when they perceived their policies as threatening.(4)

While terrorism is often associated with Islamic fundamentalism in Western perceptions, it is important to recognize the role of extremist actions on multiple sides of this conflict. The Israeli-Palestinian struggle has seen both Zionist extremists and Palestinian militants engage in violence, with civilians often caught in the crossfire. Israeli policies, shaped by certain Zionist ideologies, have led to restrictions on Arab immigration and the expansion of settlements in the West Bank, further complicating the conflict by altering demographics and limiting Palestinian rights.

The assassination of Israeli Prime Minister Yitzhak Rabin by far-right extremist Yigal Amir on November 4, 1995, underscored the deep divisions within Israeli society. This act of domestic terrorism, motivated by opposition to the Oslo Accords—a series of agreements aimed at establishing a framework for peace between Israel and the Palestine Liberation Organization (PLO)—highlighted the internal conflict within Israel itself.(5)

Understanding the complex history of violence and extremism on all sides of the conflict is crucial for comprehending the current situation and exploring potential paths toward resolution and lasting peace in the region.

Chapter# 1 The Roots of Zionism

Theodor Herzl's work Judenstaat had a profound impact on the Zionist movement worldwide. "Judenstaat" provided a clear and compelling argument for the necessity of a Jewish state, resonating with Jews worldwide who sought refuge from persecution and a place to reclaim their rights. The document ignited a sense of unity and purpose among Jewish communities, inspiring them to actively pursue the goal of establishing a homeland.

The ideas presented in Judenstaat had far-reaching consequences. They sparked widespread debate and discussion within the Jewish community, galvanizing support for the Zionist cause. Herzl's work catalyzed the subsequent establishment of various Zionist organizations and the mobilization of resources toward realizing a Jewish state.(6)

Furthermore, "Judenstaat" played a crucial role in shaping the political landscape of the time. The document initiated diplomatic efforts and negotiations with world powers to secure international recognition and support for the Zionist cause. It paved the way for future political movements and diplomatic endeavors to establish the State of Israel. The impact of the 1896 document "Judenstaat" on the Zionist movement cannot be overstated. It provided a clear vision and rationale for the pursuit of a Jewish homeland, inspiring generations of Jews to work towards the realization of this goal. The document's influence extended beyond its initial publication, shaping the course of history and laying the groundwork for establishing the modern State of Israel.

During World War I, England supported the establishment of a Jewish homeland in Palestine through the Balfour Declaration of 1917 following the Sykes-Picot Agreement of 1916. (7) The agreement, negotiated between Britain and France, aimed to divide the Middle East into distinct zones of influence for the two colonial powers.

Under Balfour Document, Britain pledged its support for creating a Jewish homeland in Palestine, alongside French control over other parts of the region. Various factors, including British strategic interests and considerations, drove this commitment.

The Interplay of British Promises and Arab Discontent

England's support for a Jewish homeland was the desire to gain the support of influential Zionist leaders and the Jewish community. England hoped that by endorsing the establishment of a Jewish homeland, it could rally Jewish support and gain leverage in its war efforts against the Ottoman Empire, which controlled Palestine at the time. England saw the Zionist movement as a potential ally in securing its regional interests. The British believed that establishing a Jewish homeland could help stabilize the area and provide a friendly presence amidst the volatile landscape of the Middle East.

The Sykes-Picot Agreement, however, was controversial. Many Arab leaders and communities were excluded from the negotiations and unaware of the agreement's details. This lack of transparency and disregard for Arab aspirations and rights ultimately led to disappointment and frustration among the Arab population. This agreement's exclusion of Arab voices and interests sowed seeds of discord that would have lasting impacts on the region.

The Sykes-Picot Agreement of 1916 and the Balfour Declaration of 1917 were two significant but initially separate elements of British policy regarding the future of the Middle East, particularly Palestine. Understanding their integration requires exploring the geopolitical and strategic considerations that influenced British decision-making during and after World War I. The Balfour Declaration was a public statement by the British government, conveyed in a letter from Foreign Secretary Arthur Balfour

https[1]://[2]www[3].[4]britannica[5].[6]com[7]/[8]event[9]/[10]Balfour[11]-[12]Declaration[13]

---

1. https://www.britannica.com/event/Balfour-Declaration

2. https://www.britannica.com/event/Balfour-Declaration

3. https://www.britannica.com/event/Balfour-Declaration

to Lord[14]Rothschild[15],[16] a leader of the British Jewish community. It expressed British support for "the establishment in Palestine of a national home for the Jewish people," provided that "nothing shall be done which may prejudice the civil and religious rights of existing non-Jewish communities in Palestine."

Strategic and Diplomatic Motives: The Balfour Declaration was partly motivated by the need to garner support from Jewish communities worldwide for the Allied war effort. Britain sought to secure the backing of influential Jewish figures in Europe and the United States. This declaration also aimed to ensure a strategic foothold in Palestine, which was crucial for maintaining British influence in the Middle East, protecting the Suez Canal, and accessing the region's emerging oil resources.

Integrating the Balfour Declaration into the British mandate system laid the groundwork for enduring conflict. The British attempt to balance the conflicting interests of Jews and Arabs proved increasingly

---

4. https://www.britannica.com/event/Balfour-Declaration

5. https://www.britannica.com/event/Balfour-Declaration

6. https://www.britannica.com/event/Balfour-Declaration

7. https://www.britannica.com/event/Balfour-Declaration

8. https://www.britannica.com/event/Balfour-Declaration

9. https://www.britannica.com/event/Balfour-Declaration

10. https://www.britannica.com/event/Balfour-Declaration

11. https://www.britannica.com/event/Balfour-Declaration

12. https://www.britannica.com/event/Balfour-Declaration

13. https://www.britannica.com/event/Balfour-Declaration

14. https://www.rothschildarchive.org/family/family_interests/
    walter_rothschild_and_the_balfour_declaration

15. https://www.rothschildarchive.org/family/family_interests/
    walter_rothschild_and_the_balfour_declaration

16. https://www.rothschildarchive.org/family/family_interests/
    walter_rothschild_and_the_balfour_declaration

untenable, leading to outbreaks of violence, such as the Arab Revolt (1936-1939), and setting the stage for the eventual partition of Palestine in 1947.

Recognizing the influence that the Zionist movement held over the Jewish population globally, Britain sought to tap into this support to bolster its war efforts. By securing the backing of the Zionists, Britain hoped not only to receive military assistance but also to rally the influential Zionist leaders behind its cause. This decision marked the beginning of a series of events that would shape the destiny of Palestine and the Middle East for years to come. Under secrecy, British officials engaged in discussions with influential Zionist leaders. They promised political recognition and support for the establishment of a Jewish homeland in Palestine, a land deeply tied to Jewish history and heritage. In return, Britain sought the Zionists' assistance in mobilizing Jewish communities worldwide to support the war efforts. The early 20th century was a period of intense struggle and aspiration for the Jewish people. The rise of the Zionist movement, propelled by the urgent need for a haven, set in motion the political and social forces that would eventually lead to the establishment of Israel. The efforts of early Zionist leaders and the critical documents they produced, such as Herzl's "Judenstaat," laid the groundwork for a national movement that sought survival and the revival of dispersed and persecuted people.

The integration of the Balfour Declaration into the broader framework of Middle Eastern governance occurred during the[17] San[18] Remo[19] Conference[20] in[21] 1920[22]. Here, the League of

---

17. https://en.wikipedia.org/wiki/

A_Peace_to_End_All_Peace#_6666cd76f96956469e7be39d750cc7d9_media_6666cd76f9695

6469e7be39d750cc7d9_File_853ae90f0351324bd73ea615e6487517_A_Peace_to_End_All_P

eace.jpg

18. https://en.wikipedia.org/wiki/

A_Peace_to_End_All_Peace#_6666cd76f96956469e7be39d750cc7d9_media_6666cd76f9695

Nations assigned mandates to Britain and France over former Ottoman territories. Britain received the Mandate for Palestine, including the explicit responsibility to implement the Balfour Declaration.

The formal text of the British[23]Mandate[24]for[25]Palestine[26], [27]approved[28]by[29]the[30]League[31]of[32]Nations[33]in[34] 1922[35], included the

6469e7be39d750cc7d9_File_853ae90f0351324bd73ea615e6487517_A_Peace_to_End_All_Peace.jpg

19. https://en.wikipedia.org/wiki/
A_Peace_to_End_All_Peace#_6666cd76f96956469e7be39d750cc7d9_media_6666cd76f9695 6469e7be39d750cc7d9_File_853ae90f0351324bd73ea615e6487517_A_Peace_to_End_All_P eace.jpg

20. https://en.wikipedia.org/wiki/
A_Peace_to_End_All_Peace#_6666cd76f96956469e7be39d750cc7d9_media_6666cd76f9695 6469e7be39d750cc7d9_File_853ae90f0351324bd73ea615e6487517_A_Peace_to_End_All_P eace.jpg

21. https://en.wikipedia.org/wiki/
A_Peace_to_End_All_Peace#_6666cd76f96956469e7be39d750cc7d9_media_6666cd76f9695 6469e7be39d750cc7d9_File_853ae90f0351324bd73ea615e6487517_A_Peace_to_End_All_P eace.jpg

22. https://en.wikipedia.org/wiki/
A_Peace_to_End_All_Peace#_6666cd76f96956469e7be39d750cc7d9_media_6666cd76f9695 6469e7be39d750cc7d9_File_853ae90f0351324bd73ea615e6487517_A_Peace_to_End_All_P eace.jpg

23. https://www.loc.gov/item/2021666887/
24. https://www.loc.gov/item/2021666887/
25. https://www.loc.gov/item/2021666887/
26. https://www.loc.gov/item/2021666887/
27. https://www.loc.gov/item/2021666887/
28. https://www.loc.gov/item/2021666887/
29. https://www.loc.gov/item/2021666887/
30. https://www.loc.gov/item/2021666887/

Balfour Declaration. This document outlined Britain's dual obligations: to facilitate the establishment of a Jewish national home and to protect the rights of the Arab population.

In the aftermath of World War I, the French had a relationship with Christians living in Lebanon, which caused tension with Syrian nationalists who opposed French control from 1920 to 1923. The Muslims in Lebanon also viewed the Maronite Christians as an enemy supported by the French.

In late June 1919, Prince[36]Faisal[37]of[38]the[39]Hussein[40]family[41] convened the Syrian National Congress.

The[42]Syrian[43]National[44]Congress[45]rejected[46]the[47]Faisal[48]-4[49]Clemenceau[50]Agreement[51] in the early 20th century. The decision

---

31. https://www.loc.gov/item/2021666887/

32. https://www.loc.gov/item/2021666887/

33. https://www.loc.gov/item/2021666887/

34. https://www.loc.gov/item/2021666887/

35. https://www.loc.gov/item/2021666887/

36. https://en.wikipedia.org/wiki/Faisal_I_of_Iraq

37. https://en.wikipedia.org/wiki/Faisal_I_of_Iraq

38. https://en.wikipedia.org/wiki/Faisal_I_of_Iraq

39. https://en.wikipedia.org/wiki/Faisal_I_of_Iraq

40. https://en.wikipedia.org/wiki/Faisal_I_of_Iraq

41. https://en.wikipedia.org/wiki/Faisal_I_of_Iraq

42. https://archive.org/details/fromparistosevre0000helm

43. https://archive.org/details/fromparistosevre0000helm

44. https://archive.org/details/fromparistosevre0000helm

45. https://archive.org/details/fromparistosevre0000helm

46. https://archive.org/details/fromparistosevre0000helm

47. https://archive.org/details/fromparistosevre0000helm

48. https://archive.org/details/fromparistosevre0000helm

49. https://archive.org/details/fromparistosevre0000helm

50. https://archive.org/details/fromparistosevre0000helm

echoed the demand for unity and independence in Syria. It marked a significant shift in their preference for the Mandate, favoring the United States and Britain over France.

The Parliament of the Levant was supposed to consist of 85 members representing various regions and communities. However, the French authorities, seeking to impose their control over the area, effectively barred Faisal's supporters from participating in the legislative process. The Syrian National Congress's rejection of the Faisal-Clemenceau Agreement and subsequent actions significantly impacted Syrian history. It sparked a series of independence movements, ultimately leading to the establishment of the Syrian Arab Republic in 1946. This was a crucial achievement for Syria, as it asserted its position as an independent nation on the global stage. The Congress's rejection of the French Mandate and its preference for an American and British mandate demonstrated its strategic knowledge of the geopolitical situation of the time. It showcased their political skills and ability to navigate complex international dynamics in their pursuit of independence.

The rationale behind this preference was the belief that these nations, particularly the United States, were more likely to respect Syrian sovereignty and allow for greater autonomy. The Syrian National Congress was also influenced by the principles of democracy and self-determination advocated by the United States, which they hoped would be applied to their cause.

The Faisal-Clemenceau Agreement, signed in 1919, was a proposal to establish a French mandate in Syria and Lebanon. The agreement was named after the two signatories, Emir Faisal of the Arab Kingdom and Georges Clemenceau, the Prime Minister of France. While the agreement was seen as a means to establish control and bring stability to the region post World War I, it was met with strong opposition from the Syrian National Congress. The Syrian National Congress

---

51. https://archive.org/details/fromparistosevre0000helm

vehemently rejected the Faisal-Clemenceau Agreement. The intense desire for a unified and independent Syria fueled the opposition. The Syrian National Congress, representing the Syrian nationalists, argued that the agreement compromised Syria's sovereignty and contradicted their aspirations for self-determination. The Congress demanded the complete independence of Syria, rejecting any form of foreign Mandate.

News of this clandestine alliance by the French and British spread among the Zionist community, sparking discussions and debates about the role they could played in shaping the course of the war. The Zionists, driven by their nationalist aspirations and the desire to secure a homeland for their people saw an opportunity to leverage their influence on a global scale. They agreed to support Britain, hoping their assistance would pave the way for realizing their dreams. However, the consequences of this alliance were more comprehensive than the immediate war efforts. The influence of the Zionists began to permeate the political landscape, both during and after the war. As Britain and its allies emerged victorious, the Zionist movement gained recognition and support from the international community.

The Balfour Declaration, a public statement issued by the British government, affirmed their commitment to establishing a Jewish homeland in Palestine.

While many Zionists celebrated the Balfour Declaration as a significant step towards realizing their aspirations, it also sparked discontent and resistance among the Arab population. The promise of a Jewish homeland in Palestine disregarded the rights and aspirations of the Arab communities already residing in the region. This imbalance of interests laid the groundwork for the Jewish-Palestinian conflict that persisted for decades.

The document ignited a sense of unity and purpose among Jewish communities, inspiring them to actively pursue the goal of establishing a homeland. The ideas presented in "Judenstaat" had far-reaching consequences. It sparked widespread debate and discussion within the Jewish community, galvanizing support for the Zionist cause.

The Zionist vision was rooted in the belief that a Jewish state would not only provide a haven for Jews but also serve as a catalyst for the cultural, social, and economic revival of the Jewish people. It aimed to unite Jews worldwide, fostering a profound sense of unity and shared purpose. At the heart of the Zionist idea was the recognition that Jews needed a sovereign state to protect their rights and preserve their identity.

The early Zionist leaders, such as **Theodor**[52]**Herzl**[53] and **Chaim**[54]**Weizmann**[55], advocated for establishing a Jewish homeland through diplomatic means and political negotiations. Their efforts laid the foundation for the eventual creation of the State of Israel in 1948.

The 1896 document "[56]**Judenhstaat**[57],"[58] " Theodor Herzl, a

---

52. https://herzlinstitute.org/en/theodor-herzl/

53. https://herzlinstitute.org/en/theodor-herzl/

54. https://zionism-israel.com/bio/Chaim_Weizmann_biography.htm

55. https://zionism-israel.com/bio/Chaim_Weizmann_biography.htm

56. https://en.wikipedia.org/wiki/
Der_Judenstaat#_853ae90f0351324bd73ea615e6487517__4c761f170e016836ff84498202
b99827__853ae90f0351324bd73ea615e6487517_text_43ec3e5dee6e706af7766fffea51272
1_Der_0bcef9c45bd8a48eda1b26eb0c61c869_20Judenstaat_0bcef9c45bd8a48eda1b26eb
0c61c869_20_84c40473414caf2ed4a7b1283e48bbf4_German_0bcef9c45bd8a48eda1b26
eb0c61c869_2C_0bcef9c45bd8a48eda1b26eb0c61c869_20lit._c0cb5f0fcf239ab3d9c1fcd
31fff1efc_Breitenstein_3590cb8af0bbb9e78c343b52b93773c9_s_0bcef9c45bd8a48eda1b
26eb0c61c869_20Verlags_0bcef9c45bd8a48eda1b26eb0c61c869_2DBuchhandlung.

57. https://en.wikipedia.org/wiki/
Der_Judenstaat#_853ae90f0351324bd73ea615e6487517__4c761f170e016836ff84498202
b99827__853ae90f0351324bd73ea615e6487517_text_43ec3e5dee6e706af7766fffea51272
1_Der_0bcef9c45bd8a48eda1b26eb0c61c869_20Judenstaat_0bcef9c45bd8a48eda1b26eb
0c61c869_20_84c40473414caf2ed4a7b1283e48bbf4_German_0bcef9c45bd8a48eda1b26
eb0c61c869_2C_0bcef9c45bd8a48eda1b26eb0c61c869_20lit._c0cb5f0fcf239ab3d9c1fcd

prominent figure in the early Zionist movement, presented a comprehensive vision for establishing a Jewish homeland. In "Judenstaat," Herzl argued that the persistent persecution and discrimination against Jews necessitated the creation of a sovereign Jewish state. He proposed that Jews should actively pursue the acquisition of a territory where they could live freely and independently.

Additionally, England saw the Zionist movement as a potential ally in securing its interests in the region. The British believed that establishing a Jewish homeland could help stabilize the area and provide a friendly presence amidst the volatile geopolitical landscape of the Middle East. The Sykes-Picot agreement, however, was subject to controversy. Many Arab leaders and communities were excluded from the negotiations and were unaware of the agreement's details. This lack of transparency and disregard for Arab aspirations and rights ultimately led to disappointment and frustration among the Arab population.

Chapter # 2

The meaning of the Sykes Picot agreement and the Balfour document in Palestine 1920

This agreement, negotiated between Britain and France, aimed to divide the Middle East into distinct zones of influence for the two

---

31fff1efc_Breitenstein_3590cb8af0bbb9e78c343b52b93773c9_s_0bcef9c45bd8a48eda1b26eb0c61c869_20Verlags_0bcef9c45bd8a48eda1b26eb0c61c869_2DBuchhandlung.

58. https://en.wikipedia.org/wiki/

Der_Judenstaat#_853ae90f0351324bd73ea615e6487517__4c761f170e016836ff84498202b99827__853ae90f0351324bd73ea615e6487517_text_43ec3e5dee6e706af7766fffea512721_Der_0bcef9c45bd8a48eda1b26eb0c61c869_20Judenstaat_0bcef9c45bd8a48eda1b26eb0c61c869_20_84c40473414caf2ed4a7b1283e48bbf4_German_0bcef9c45bd8a48eda1b26eb0c61c869_2C_0bcef9c45bd8a48eda1b26eb0c61c869_20lit._c0cb5f0fcf239ab3d9c1fcd31fff1efc_Breitenstein_3590cb8af0bbb9e78c343b52b93773c9_s_0bcef9c45bd8a48eda1b26eb0c61c869_20Verlags_0bcef9c45bd8a48eda1b26eb0c61c869_2DBuchhandlung.

colonial powers. Under the Sykes-Picot agreement, Britain pledged its support for the creation of a Jewish homeland in Palestine, alongside French control over other parts of the region. Various factors, including British strategic interests and geopolitical considerations, drove this commitment. One significant factor behind England's support for a Jewish homeland was the desire to gain the support of influential Zionist leaders and the Jewish community. England hoped that by endorsing the establishment of a Jewish homeland, it could rally Jewish support and gain leverage in its war efforts against the Ottoman Empire, which controlled Palestine at the time.

England saw the Zionist movement as a potential ally in securing its regional interests. The British believed that establishing a Jewish homeland could help stabilize the area and provide a friendly presence amidst the volatile landscape of the Middle East. The Sykes-Picot agreement, however, was subject to controversy. Many Arab leaders and communities were excluded from the negotiations and were unaware of the agreement's details.

This lack of transparency and disregard for Arab aspirations and rights ultimately led to disappointment and frustration among the Arab population. The Sykes-Picot agreement contradicted the promises of self-determination made by the British during the war, particularly to Arab leaders who were promised independence in exchange for their support against the Ottoman Empire. The agreement's division of the region into zones of influence for colonial powers undermined these promises and fueled resentment among Arab nationalists.

The Sykes-Picot agreement marked England's support for establishing a Jewish homeland in Palestine during World War I. Strategic interests drove this support, as did the desire to gain Jewish support and the belief that a Jewish presence could help stabilize the region.

The Sykes-Picot agreement contradicted the British promises of self-determination during the war, particularly to Arab leaders who were promised independence in exchange for their support against the

Ottoman Empire. The agreement's division of the region into zones of influence for colonial powers undermined these promises and fueled resentment among Arab nationalists.

The French were particularly interested in securing control over present-day Syria and Lebanon areas. Britain and France sought to maintain the balance of power in the region by preventing any single power from gaining too much control. The agreement aimed to divide the Middle East into spheres of influence, with each colonial power exerting control over designated territories. However, the expectations of the Russians and Italians regarding the Sykes-Picot agreement still needed to be fully met. The Russians, who were part of the Allied powers, expected to have a say in the division of the Middle East.

However, they were excluded from the negotiations due to the Russian Revolution and subsequent political turmoil. Similarly, the Italians, also part of the Allied powers, were expected to be involved in the post-war division of territories.

However, they were disappointed that their interests were limitedly represented in the Sykes-Picot agreement. Italy gained southern Anatolia through the Agreement of Saint-Jean-de-Maurienne from the Sykes-Picot agreement. France and Great Britain promised to give Italy. The 1919 [59]Paris[60]Peace[61]Conference[62] for Greece overturned the plans made in Sykes-Picot, and Greece obtained Izmir.

This secret agreement had significant implications for the future of Palestine and the region's geopolitical landscape. According to the Sykes-Picot Agreement, Palestine was designated as an international administration, meaning it would be governed by an international body rather than under the direct control of either Britain or France. This decision was influenced by the historical and religious

---

59. https://en.wikipedia.org/wiki/Agreement_of_Saint-Jean-de-Maurienne

60. https://en.wikipedia.org/wiki/Agreement_of_Saint-Jean-de-Maurienne

61. https://en.wikipedia.org/wiki/Agreement_of_Saint-Jean-de-Maurienne

62. https://en.wikipedia.org/wiki/Agreement_of_Saint-Jean-de-Maurienne

significance of Palestine, which held deep ties to various communities, including Jews, Muslims, and Christians. Under the agreement, other regions in the Middle East were divided between Britain and France. The areas that would belong to Britain included Mesopotamia (present-day Iraq) and Jordan. At the same time, France would control Syria and Lebanon. Strategic interests and geopolitical considerations, including access to valuable resources such as oil and preserving colonial influence in the region, drove these divisions. The importance of these regions to Britain and France was twofold. First, both countries sought to secure valuable resources, such as oil, which was abundant in Mesopotamia and other parts of the Middle East. The discovery and exploitation of oil reserves had become a strategic priority for Britain as it sought to meet its growing energy needs and maintain its global influence. Second, the Sykes-Picot Agreement aimed to preserve the balance of power between Britain and France in the region. By dividing the Middle East into distinct zones of influence, the agreement sought to prevent either country from gaining too much control and dominance. This was especially relevant in light of the declining Ottoman Empire, which had previously controlled much of the region. Control of Mesopotamia (Modern-Day Iraq)

One of Britain's primary objectives was to secure control over Mesopotamia, including Basra and Mosul's oil-rich areas. The discovery of significant oil reserves in Persia (modern-day Iran) in 1908 by the Anglo-Persian Oil Company (later British Petroleum) underscored the strategic importance of securing additional oil supplies for the Royal Navy and British industries. **Basra**: Britain aimed to control the Shatt al-Arab waterway by securing Basra, which was vital for oil transportation from Persia to the Persian Gulf. This control also provided: A critical link to India. The jewel in the British colonial crown.

Mosul was allocated to the French sphere under the Sykes-Picot Agreement. However, post-World War I negotiations saw Britain successfully lobbying for control over Mosul due to its potential oil reserves. The 1920 Treaty of Sèvres and subsequent agreements confirmed British control over Mosul, reflecting the strategic shift driven by oil interests.

The declaration also aimed to secure a strategic foothold in Palestine, crucial for maintaining British influence in the Middle East, protecting the Suez Canal, and accessing the region's emerging oil resources. The integration of the Balfour Declaration into the broader framework of Middle Eastern governance occurred during the San Remo Conference. The League of Nations assigned mandates to Britain and France over former Ottoman territories. Britain received the Mandate for Palestine, including the explicit responsibility to implement the Balfour Declaration. The formal text of the British Mandate for Palestine, approved by the League of Nations, included the Balfour Declaration. This document outlined Britain's dual obligations: to facilitate the establishment of a Jewish national home and to protect the rights of the Arab population. Integrating the Balfour Declaration into the British mandate system laid the groundwork for enduring conflict. The British attempted to balance the conflicting interests into the broader framework of Middle Eastern governance that occurred during the San Remo Conference.

The League of Nations assigned mandates to Britain and France over former Ottoman territories. Britain received the Mandate for Palestine, including the explicit responsibility to implement the Balfour Declaration. The formal text of the British Mandate for Palestine, approved by the League of Nations, included the Balfour Declaration.

In addition to direct control over oil fields, Britain was keen on securing transportation routes for oil. A priority was the construction of pipelines from the oil fields in Iraq to the Mediterranean Sea. These pipelines would facilitate efficient oil transport to Europe, bypassing the longer sea route around the Arabian Peninsula.

The port of Haifa in Palestine became a strategic asset for Britain, providing a terminal for the oil pipelines from Iraq. The development of the Haifa refinery further integrated this region into Britain's oil supply chain.

Control over Trans-Jordan (modern-day Jordan) ensured the security of overland routes and pipelines, providing a buffer zone against potential regional instability.

The declaration also aimed to secure a strategic foothold in Palestine, crucial for maintaining British influence in the Middle East, protecting the Suez Canal, and accessing the region's emerging oil resources. The integration of the Balfour Declaration into the broader framework of Middle Eastern governance occurred during the San Remo Conference. The League of Nations assigned mandates to Britain and France over former Ottoman territories. Britain received the Mandate for Palestine, including the explicit responsibility to implement the Balfour Declaration.

The formal text of the British Mandate for Palestine, approved by the League of Nations, included the Balfour Declaration. This document outlined Britain's dual obligations: to facilitate the establishment of a Jewish national home and to protect the rights of the Arab population.

This decision was influenced by the historical and religious significance of Palestine, which held deep ties to various communities, including Jews, Muslims, and Christians. Under the agreement, other regions in the Middle East were divided between Britain and France.

The areas that would belong to Britain included Mesopotamia (present-day Iraq) and Jordan. At the same time, France would control Syria and Lebanon. Strategic interests and geopolitical considerations, including access to valuable resources such as oil and preserving colonial influence in the region, drove these divisions. The importance of these regions to Britain and France was twofold. First, both countries sought to secure valuable resources, such as oil, which was abundant in Mesopotamia. They also sought to control the political climate of the political leadership.

Reactions to the Balfour Declaration and Sykes-Picot Agreement in Palestine.

The Balfour Declaration, issued by the British government in 1917, promised to support the establishment of a Jewish homeland in Palestine.

The Zionist movement, driven by nationalistic aspirations and the desire for a Jewish homeland, gained significant influence and support from the international community.

Arab nationalists began to organize politically, forming groups such as the Muslim-Christian Associations that opposed the British Mandate and Zionist immigration. These associations held congresses, such as the First Palestine Arab Congress in 1919, which unequivocally rejected the Balfour Declaration and demanded independence.

Britain's reactions to the Balfour Declaration and the Sykes-Picot Agreement were mixed. While the government and many political leaders supported the establishment of a Jewish national home, there was significant debate and opposition within political and public circles.

Critics of the Balfour Declaration, including some British politicians and public figures, argued that it contradicted promises made to the Arabs and would lead to instability and conflict. Prominent figures such as Edwin[63]Montagu[64], [65]the[66]Secretary[67]of[68]State[69]for[70]India[71],

---

63. https://liberalhistory.org.uk/history/montagu-edwin/

64. https://liberalhistory.org.uk/history/montagu-edwin/

65. https://liberalhistory.org.uk/history/montagu-edwin/

66. https://liberalhistory.org.uk/history/montagu-edwin/

[72]expressed concern that the declaration would foster anti-Semitism and jeopardize British interests in the Middle East.

Recognizing the influence that the Zionist movement held over the Jewish population globally, Britain sought to tap into this support to bolster its war efforts. By securing the backing of the Zionists, Britain hoped not only to receive military assistance but also to rally the influential Zionist leaders behind its cause. This decision marked the beginning of a series of events that would shape the destiny of Palestine and the Middle East for years to come. Under secrecy, British officials engaged in discussions with influential Zionist leaders. They promised political recognition and support for the establishment of a Jewish homeland in Palestine, a land deeply tied to Jewish history and heritage. In return, Britain sought the Zionists' assistance in mobilizing Jewish communities worldwide to support the war efforts. The Zionists, driven by their nationalist aspirations and the desire to secure a homeland for their people, saw an opportunity to leverage their influence on a global scale. They agreed to support Britain, hoping their assistance would pave the way for realizing their dreams. However, the consequences of this alliance were more comprehensive than the past war efforts.

The Zionists' influence permeated the political landscape during and after the war. As Britain and its allies emerged victorious, the Zionist movement gained recognition and support from the international community. The Balfour Declaration, a public statement issued by the British government, affirmed their commitment to establishing a Jewish homeland in Palestine. While many Zionists celebrated the

---

67. https://liberalhistory.org.uk/history/montagu-edwin/

68. https://liberalhistory.org.uk/history/montagu-edwin/

69. https://liberalhistory.org.uk/history/montagu-edwin/

70. https://liberalhistory.org.uk/history/montagu-edwin/

71. https://liberalhistory.org.uk/history/montagu-edwin/

72. https://liberalhistory.org.uk/history/montagu-edwin/

Balfour Declaration as a significant step towards realizing their aspirations, it also sparked discontent and resistance among the Arab population.

CHAPTER#3

The British Mandate of 1922.

The 1900s and the Zionist movement in Europe. During World War I, England expressed its support for the establishment of a Jewish homeland in Palestine through the Sykes-Picot agreement, signed in 1916. This agreement, negotiated between Britain and France, aimed to divide the Middle East into distinct zones of influence for the two colonial powers. Under the Sykes-Picot agreement, Britain pledged its support for the creation of a Jewish homeland in Palestine, alongside French control over other lands of the Ottoman Empire. Various factors, including British strategic interests and geopolitical considerations, drove this commitment. One significant factor behind England's support for a Jewish homeland was the desire to gain the support of influential Zionist leaders and the Jewish community. England hoped that by endorsing the establishment of a Jewish homeland, it could rally Jewish support and gain leverage in its war efforts against the Ottoman Empire, which controlled Palestine at the time.

England saw the Zionist movement as a potential ally in securing its regional interests. The British believed that promising the establishing of a Jewish homeland in Palestine could help stabilize the area and provide a friendly presence amidst the volatile political landscape of Muslim Arabs in the Middle East. The Sykes-Picot agreement, however, was subject to controversy. Many Arab leaders and communities were excluded from the negotiations and were unaware of the agreement's details. This lack of transparency and disregard for Arab aspirations and rights ultimately led to disappointment and frustration among the Arab population.

The Sykes-Picot agreement contradicted the promises of self-determination made by the British during the war, particularly to Arab leaders who were promised independence in exchange for their support against the Ottoman Empire. The agreement's division of the region into zones of influence for colonial powers undermined these promises and fueled resentment among Arab nationalists. The Sykes-Picot agreement marked England's support for establishing a Jewish homeland in Palestine after World War I ended. Strategic interests drove this support, the desire to gain Jewish support, and the belief that a Jewish presence could help stabilize the region. The British Mandate controlled the immigration that Zionist leaders expected from it and angered the Arab Nationalists who resented Jews being able to settle their land.

One significant factor behind England's support for a Jewish homeland was the desire to gain the backing of influential Zionist leaders and the global Jewish community. England believed that by endorsing the establishment of a Jewish homeland, it could secure Jewish support, particularly in its war efforts against the Ottoman Empire, which controlled Palestine at the time. However, the actual terms of the British Mandate, established after the Sykes-Picot Agreement, contained specific policies that neither Jewish nor Arab communities fully understood. The Mandate imposed British control over key areas of governance, immigration, and land ownership, creating tensions between the two groups. These policies, often perceived as conflicting promises to both sides, laid the groundwork for long-term disputes, as both Jews and Arabs felt misled by British actions and unaware of the true extent of the agreements being made behind closed doors.

France aimed to expand its colonial empire and enhance its regional influence. The French were particularly interested in securing control over present-day Syria and Lebanon areas. Britain and France sought to maintain the balance of power in the region by preventing any single power from gaining too much control. The agreement aimed to divide the Middle East into spheres of influence, with each colonial power exerting territories.

The Sykes-Picot agreement ensured British and French control over the Middle East and its valuable resources.

The Sykes-Picot Agreement, signed in 1916 between Britain and France during World War I, aimed to divide the Middle East into distinct zones of influence for the two colonial powers. This secret agreement had significant implications for Palestine's future and the region's geopolitical landscape. According to the Sykes-Picot Agreement, Jerusalem was designated as an international administration, meaning it would be governed by an international body rather than under the direct control of either Britain or France.

This decision was influenced by the historical and religious significance of Palestine, which held deep ties to various communities, including Jews, Muslims, and Christians. Under the agreement, other regions in the Middle East were divided between Britain and France only.

The areas that would belong to Britain included Mesopotamia (present-day Iraq) and Jordan. At the same time, France would control Syria and Lebanon. Strategic interests and geopolitical considerations, including access to valuable resources such as oil and preserving colonial influence in the region, drove these divisions. The importance of these regions to Britain and France was twofold. First, both countries sought to secure valuable resources, such as oil from Britain and the passage of the Suez Canal.

The discovery and exploitation of oil reserves had become a strategic priority for Britain as it sought to meet its growing energy needs and maintain its global influence. The Sykes-Picot Agreement aimed to preserve the balance of power between Britain and France in the region. By dividing the Middle East into distinct zones of influence, the agreement sought to prevent either country from gaining too much control and dominance. This was especially relevant in light of the declining Ottoman Empire, which had previously controlled much of the region.

One of Britain's primary objectives was to secure control over Mesopotamia, including Basra and Mosul's oil-rich areas. The discovery of significant oil reserves in Persia (modern-day Iran) in 1908 by the Anglo-Persian Oil Company (later British Petroleum) underscored the strategic importance of securing additional oil supplies for the Royal Navy and British industries.

Britain aimed to control the Shatt al-Arab waterway by securing Basra, which was vital for oil transportation from Persia to the Persian Gulf. This control also provided

A critical link to India. This was one of Britain's most important military safeguards.

Initially, Mosul was allocated to the French under the Sykes-Picot Agreement. However, post-World War I negotiations saw Britain successfully lobbying for control over Mosul due to its potential oil reserves. The[73] 1920 [74]Treaty[75]of[76]Sèvres[77] and subsequent agreements confirmed British control over Mosul, reflecting the strategic shift driven by oil interests.

Securing Transportation Routes

In addition to direct control over oil fields, Britain was keen on securing transportation routes for oil. A priority was the construction of pipelines from the oil fields in Iraq to the Mediterranean Sea. These

---

73. http://net.lib.byu.edu/~rdh7/wwi/versa/sevres1.html

74. http://net.lib.byu.edu/~rdh7/wwi/versa/sevres1.html

75. http://net.lib.byu.edu/~rdh7/wwi/versa/sevres1.html

76. http://net.lib.byu.edu/~rdh7/wwi/versa/sevres1.html

77. http://net.lib.byu.edu/~rdh7/wwi/versa/sevres1.html

pipelines would facilitate efficient oil transport to Europe, bypassing the longer sea route around the Arabian Peninsula.

The port of Haifa in Palestine became a strategic asset obtained away from France by Britain. It provided a terminal for the oil pipeline from Iraq. The development of the Haifa refinery further integrated this region into Britain's oil supply chain.

Control over Trans-Jordan (modern-day Jordan) ensured the security of overland routes and pipelines, providing a buffer zone against potential regional instability.

Beyond economic interests, Britain's control over these regions allowed it to exert significant influence in the Middle East. This control helped counterbalance French ambitions to maintain regional stability and safeguard the approaches to the Suez Canal, a vital artery for British maritime trade and military logistics.

The initial reaction among the Arab population in Palestine to the Balfour Declaration and the Sykes-Picot Agreement was that supporting the British against the Ottoman Empire would give their leaders control of their regions. Many Arabs had been led to believe that their support for the Allies during World War I would establish independent Arab states, as implied by the correspondence between Sharif[78] Hussein[79] of[80] Mecca[81] and Sir[82] Henry[83] McMahon[84].[85]

As the implications of the Balfour Declaration became clearer, opposition grew. Arab leaders and intellectuals organized protests and articulated their grievances, emphasizing the incompatibility of the

78. https://en.wikipedia.org/wiki/Hussein_bin_Ali,_King_of_Hejaz

79. https://en.wikipedia.org/wiki/Hussein_bin_Ali,_King_of_Hejaz

80. https://en.wikipedia.org/wiki/Hussein_bin_Ali,_King_of_Hejaz

81. https://en.wikipedia.org/wiki/Hussein_bin_Ali,_King_of_Hejaz

82. https://en.wikipedia.org/wiki/McMahon%E2%80%93Hussein_correspondence

83. https://en.wikipedia.org/wiki/McMahon%E2%80%93Hussein_correspondence

84. https://en.wikipedia.org/wiki/McMahon%E2%80%93Hussein_correspondence

85. https://en.wikipedia.org/wiki/McMahon%E2%80%93Hussein_correspondence

establishment of a Jewish national home with the political and national aspirations of the Arab majority in Palestine. Arab nationalists began to organize politically, forming groups such as the[86]Muslim[87]-[88]Christian[89]Associations[90] that opposed the British

---

86. https://en.wikipedia.org/wiki/

Muslim-Christian_Associations#_853ae90f0351324bd73ea615e6487517__4c761f170e01683 6ff84498202b99827__853ae90f0351324bd73ea615e6487517_text_43ec3e5dee6e706af7766ff fea512721_The_0bcef9c45bd8a48eda1b26eb0c61c869_20Muslim_0bcef9c45bd8a48eda1b26 eb0c61c869_2DChristian_0bcef9c45bd8a48eda1b26eb0c61c869_20Associations_0bcef9c45b d8a48eda1b26eb0c61c869_20are_c0cb5f0fcf239ab3d9c1fcd31fff1efc_had_0bcef9c45bd8a48e da1b26eb0c61c869_20ceased_0bcef9c45bd8a48eda1b26eb0c61c869_20to_0bcef9c45bd8a48 eda1b26eb0c61c869_20be_0bcef9c45bd8a48eda1b26eb0c61c869_20important.

87. https://en.wikipedia.org/wiki/

Muslim-Christian_Associations#_853ae90f0351324bd73ea615e6487517__4c761f170e01683 6ff84498202b99827__853ae90f0351324bd73ea615e6487517_text_43ec3e5dee6e706af7766ff fea512721_The_0bcef9c45bd8a48eda1b26eb0c61c869_20Muslim_0bcef9c45bd8a48eda1b26 eb0c61c869_2DChristian_0bcef9c45bd8a48eda1b26eb0c61c869_20Associations_0bcef9c45b d8a48eda1b26eb0c61c869_20are_c0cb5f0fcf239ab3d9c1fcd31fff1efc_had_0bcef9c45bd8a48e da1b26eb0c61c869_20ceased_0bcef9c45bd8a48eda1b26eb0c61c869_20to_0bcef9c45bd8a48 eda1b26eb0c61c869_20be_0bcef9c45bd8a48eda1b26eb0c61c869_20important.

88. https://en.wikipedia.org/wiki/

Muslim-Christian_Associations#_853ae90f0351324bd73ea615e6487517__4c761f170e01683 6ff84498202b99827__853ae90f0351324bd73ea615e6487517_text_43ec3e5dee6e706af7766ff fea512721_The_0bcef9c45bd8a48eda1b26eb0c61c869_20Muslim_0bcef9c45bd8a48eda1b26 eb0c61c869_2DChristian_0bcef9c45bd8a48eda1b26eb0c61c869_20Associations_0bcef9c45b d8a48eda1b26eb0c61c869_20are_c0cb5f0fcf239ab3d9c1fcd31fff1efc_had_0bcef9c45bd8a48e da1b26eb0c61c869_20ceased_0bcef9c45bd8a48eda1b26eb0c61c869_20to_0bcef9c45bd8a48 eda1b26eb0c61c869_20be_0bcef9c45bd8a48eda1b26eb0c61c869_20important.

89. https://en.wikipedia.org/wiki/

Muslim-Christian_Associations#_853ae90f0351324bd73ea615e6487517__4c761f170e01683 6ff84498202b99827__853ae90f0351324bd73ea615e6487517_text_43ec3e5dee6e706af7766ff fea512721_The_0bcef9c45bd8a48eda1b26eb0c61c869_20Muslim_0bcef9c45bd8a48eda1b26

Mandate and Zionist immigration. These associations held congresses, such as the First[91]Palestine[92]Arab[93]Congress[94]in[95] 1919[96], which

eb0c61c869_2DChristian_0bcef9c45bd8a48eda1b26eb0c61c869_20Associations_0bcef9c45b

d8a48eda1b26eb0c61c869_20are_c0cb5f0fcf239ab3d9c1fcd31fff1efc_had_0bcef9c45bd8a48e

da1b26eb0c61c869_20ceased_0bcef9c45bd8a48eda1b26eb0c61c869_20to_0bcef9c45bd8a48

eda1b26eb0c61c869_20be_0bcef9c45bd8a48eda1b26eb0c61c869_20important.

90. https://en.wikipedia.org/wiki/

Muslim-Christian_Associations#_853ae90f0351324bd73ea615e6487517__4c761f170e01683

6ff84498202b99827__853ae90f0351324bd73ea615e6487517_text_43ec3e5dee6e706af7766ff

fea512721_The_0bcef9c45bd8a48eda1b26eb0c61c869_20Muslim_0bcef9c45bd8a48eda1b26

eb0c61c869_2DChristian_0bcef9c45bd8a48eda1b26eb0c61c869_20Associations_0bcef9c45b

d8a48eda1b26eb0c61c869_20are_c0cb5f0fcf239ab3d9c1fcd31fff1efc_had_0bcef9c45bd8a48e

da1b26eb0c61c869_20ceased_0bcef9c45bd8a48eda1b26eb0c61c869_20to_0bcef9c45bd8a48

eda1b26eb0c61c869_20be_0bcef9c45bd8a48eda1b26eb0c61c869_20important.

91. https://en.wikipedia.org/wiki/

Palestine_Arab_Congress#_853ae90f0351324bd73ea615e6487517__4c761f170e016836ff844

98202b99827__853ae90f0351324bd73ea615e6487517_text_43ec3e5dee6e706af7766fffea512

721_In_0bcef9c45bd8a48eda1b26eb0c61c869_20response_0bcef9c45bd8a48eda1b26eb0c61c

869_20to_0bcef9c45bd8a48eda1b26eb0c61c869_20Jewish_0bcef9c45bd8a48eda1b26eb0c61

c869_20immigrants_c0cb5f0fcf239ab3d9c1fcd31fff1efc_the_0bcef9c45bd8a48eda1b26eb0c6

1c869_20Jerusalem_0bcef9c45bd8a48eda1b26eb0c61c869_20Muslim_0bcef9c45bd8a48eda1

b26eb0c61c869_2DChristian_0bcef9c45bd8a48eda1b26eb0c61c869_20Society.

92. https://en.wikipedia.org/wiki/

Palestine_Arab_Congress#_853ae90f0351324bd73ea615e6487517__4c761f170e016836ff844

98202b99827__853ae90f0351324bd73ea615e6487517_text_43ec3e5dee6e706af7766fffea512

721_In_0bcef9c45bd8a48eda1b26eb0c61c869_20response_0bcef9c45bd8a48eda1b26eb0c61c

869_20to_0bcef9c45bd8a48eda1b26eb0c61c869_20Jewish_0bcef9c45bd8a48eda1b26eb0c61

c869_20immigrants_c0cb5f0fcf239ab3d9c1fcd31fff1efc_the_0bcef9c45bd8a48eda1b26eb0c6

1c869_20Jerusalem_0bcef9c45bd8a48eda1b26eb0c61c869_20Muslim_0bcef9c45bd8a48eda1

b26eb0c61c869_2DChristian_0bcef9c45bd8a48eda1b26eb0c61c869_20Society.

93. https://en.wikipedia.org/wiki/

Palestine_Arab_Congress#_853ae90f0351324bd73ea615e6487517__4c761f170e016836ff844 unequivocally rejected the Balfour Declaration and demanded independence. (13)

98202b99827__853ae90f0351324bd73ea615e6487517_text_43ec3e5dee6e706af7766fffea512721_In_0bcef9c45bd8a48eda1b26eb0c61c869_20response_0bcef9c45bd8a48eda1b26eb0c61c869_20to_0bcef9c45bd8a48eda1b26eb0c61c869_20Jewish_0bcef9c45bd8a48eda1b26eb0c61c869_20immigrants_c0cb5f0fcf239ab3d9c1fcd31fff1efc_the_0bcef9c45bd8a48eda1b26eb0c61c869_20Jerusalem_0bcef9c45bd8a48eda1b26eb0c61c869_20Muslim_0bcef9c45bd8a48eda1b26eb0c61c869_2DChristian_0bcef9c45bd8a48eda1b26eb0c61c869_20Society.

94. https://en.wikipedia.org/wiki/

Palestine_Arab_Congress#_853ae90f0351324bd73ea615e6487517__4c761f170e016836ff84498202b99827__853ae90f0351324bd73ea615e6487517_text_43ec3e5dee6e706af7766fffea512721_In_0bcef9c45bd8a48eda1b26eb0c61c869_20response_0bcef9c45bd8a48eda1b26eb0c61c869_20to_0bcef9c45bd8a48eda1b26eb0c61c869_20Jewish_0bcef9c45bd8a48eda1b26eb0c61c869_20immigrants_c0cb5f0fcf239ab3d9c1fcd31fff1efc_the_0bcef9c45bd8a48eda1b26eb0c61c869_20Jerusalem_0bcef9c45bd8a48eda1b26eb0c61c869_20Muslim_0bcef9c45bd8a48eda1b26eb0c61c869_2DChristian_0bcef9c45bd8a48eda1b26eb0c61c869_20Society.

95. https://en.wikipedia.org/wiki/

Palestine_Arab_Congress#_853ae90f0351324bd73ea615e6487517__4c761f170e016836ff84498202b99827__853ae90f0351324bd73ea615e6487517_text_43ec3e5dee6e706af7766fffea512721_In_0bcef9c45bd8a48eda1b26eb0c61c869_20response_0bcef9c45bd8a48eda1b26eb0c61c869_20to_0bcef9c45bd8a48eda1b26eb0c61c869_20Jewish_0bcef9c45bd8a48eda1b26eb0c61c869_20immigrants_c0cb5f0fcf239ab3d9c1fcd31fff1efc_the_0bcef9c45bd8a48eda1b26eb0c61c869_20Jerusalem_0bcef9c45bd8a48eda1b26eb0c61c869_20Muslim_0bcef9c45bd8a48eda1b26eb0c61c869_2DChristian_0bcef9c45bd8a48eda1b26eb0c61c869_20Society.

96. https://en.wikipedia.org/wiki/

Palestine_Arab_Congress#_853ae90f0351324bd73ea615e6487517__4c761f170e016836ff84498202b99827__853ae90f0351324bd73ea615e6487517_text_43ec3e5dee6e706af7766fffea512721_In_0bcef9c45bd8a48eda1b26eb0c61c869_20response_0bcef9c45bd8a48eda1b26eb0c61c869_20to_0bcef9c45bd8a48eda1b26eb0c61c869_20Jewish_0bcef9c45bd8a48eda1b26eb0c61c869_20immigrants_c0cb5f0fcf239ab3d9c1fcd31fff1efc_the_0bcef9c45bd8a48eda1b26eb0c61c869_20Jerusalem_0bcef9c45bd8a48eda1b26eb0c61c869_20Muslim_0bcef9c45bd8a48eda1b26eb0c61c869_2DChristian_0bcef9c45bd8a48eda1b26eb0c61c869_20Society.

Britain's reactions to the Balfour Declaration and the Sykes-Picot Agreement were mixed. While the government and many political leaders supported the establishment of a Jewish national home, there was significant debate and opposition within political and public circles.

Critics of the Balfour Declaration, including some British politicians and public figures, argued that it contradicted promises made to the Arabs and would lead to instability and conflict. Prominent figures such as Edwin[97]Montagu[98], the Secretary of State for India, expressed concern that the declaration would foster anti-Semitism and jeopardize British interests in the Middle East.

The growing conflict in Palestine and the broader Middle East challenged British strategic interests, particularly regarding access to oil resources and maintaining stability in the region. The British government had to navigate the competing demands of Zionist and Arab nationalist movements while safeguarding its economic interests.

CHAPTER #4

The Franco-Syrian War 1920

Henri[99]Gouraud[100] was aFrench[101] general best known for leading theFrench[102]Fourth[103]Army[104] at the end of theFirst[105]World[106]War[107]. He became the firstHigh[108]Commissioner[109]of[110]the[111]Levant[112]

---

97. https://www.britannica.com/biography/Edwin-Samuel-Montagu

98. https://www.britannica.com/biography/Edwin-Samuel-Montagu

99. https://en.wikipedia.org/wiki/Henri_Gouraud

100. https://en.wikipedia.org/wiki/Henri_Gouraud

101. https://en.wikipedia.org/wiki/French_people

102. https://en.wikipedia.org/wiki/Fourth_Army_(France)

103. https://en.wikipedia.org/wiki/Fourth_Army_(France)

104. https://en.wikipedia.org/wiki/Fourth_Army_(France)

105. https://en.wikipedia.org/wiki/First_World_War

106. https://en.wikipedia.org/wiki/First_World_War

107. https://en.wikipedia.org/wiki/First_World_War

(1919–1922). He controlled the region that the Mandate gave France as a part of the Sykes-Picot Agreement. He demanded that King Faisal I of Syria give up the control given to him following his support of the British in defeating the Ottoman Empire. Faisal surrendered to General Gouraud to prevent a blood bath for his people. (14) King Faisal hoped that the Americans and the British would preserve his power. However, the Anglo-French Agreement provided for the withdrawal of British troops from Syria, signaling the end of British military involvement in Syria.

Minister[113] of[114] Defence[115] Yusuf[116] al[117]-[118] Azma[119] refused to surrender control to the French and led a group of men to fight the French and their supporters. On July 24, 1920, the Battle of Maysalun began; when the French artillery began to overcome the Syrian artillery,

108. https://en.wikipedia.org/wiki/High_Commissioner_of_the_Levant

109. https://en.wikipedia.org/wiki/High_Commissioner_of_the_Levant

110. https://en.wikipedia.org/wiki/High_Commissioner_of_the_Levant

111. https://en.wikipedia.org/wiki/High_Commissioner_of_the_Levant

112. https://en.wikipedia.org/wiki/High_Commissioner_of_the_Levant

113. https://www.google.com/books/edition/
Faisal_I_of_Iraq/_t_AAgAAQBAJ?hl=en&gbpv=1&pg=PA287&printsec=frontcover

114. https://www.google.com/books/edition/
Faisal_I_of_Iraq/_t_AAgAAQBAJ?hl=en&gbpv=1&pg=PA287&printsec=frontcover

115. https://www.google.com/books/edition/
Faisal_I_of_Iraq/_t_AAgAAQBAJ?hl=en&gbpv=1&pg=PA287&printsec=frontcover

116. https://www.google.com/books/edition/
Faisal_I_of_Iraq/_t_AAgAAQBAJ?hl=en&gbpv=1&pg=PA287&printsec=frontcover

117. https://www.google.com/books/edition/
Faisal_I_of_Iraq/_t_AAgAAQBAJ?hl=en&gbpv=1&pg=PA287&printsec=frontcover

118. https://www.google.com/books/edition/
Faisal_I_of_Iraq/_t_AAgAAQBAJ?hl=en&gbpv=1&pg=PA287&printsec=frontcover

119. https://www.google.com/books/edition/
Faisal_I_of_Iraq/_t_AAgAAQBAJ?hl=en&gbpv=1&pg=PA287&printsec=frontcover

French tanks started advancing toward the front line of the defending forces. French Senegalese soldiers started attacking the left side of the Syrian Army. However, Yussuf al-Azma was killed by the superior forces of the French military in the battle on July 24, 1920.

The battle of Maysalun led to the surrender of the Syrian forces, resulting in French control of the region. (15)

Recognizing the futility of further resistance, King Faisal decided to comply with the French demands to prevent further bloodshed and devastation. His pragmatic decision aimed to safeguard the Syrian population from the wrath of the victorious French forces.

Faisal left Damascus on July 25, 1920, the day after the Battle of Maysalun. This marked the end of his short-lived reign over the Arab Kingdom of Syria.

The British, who had supported Faisal during the Arab Revolt against the Ottoman Empire, played a role in his future political career, recognizing his leadership and the symbolic importance of his role in the Arab nationalist movement.

1921, with British support, Faisal was installed as the King of Iraq. This move was part of a broader British strategy to stabilize the region and ensure a friendly regime in Iraq. Faisal's experience and leadership were assets in governing the newly established Kingdom of Iraq.

His pragmatic decision to avoid further confrontation with the French ultimately led to his relocation and new role as the King of Iraq, where he continued to influence the course of Arab nationalism and state-building.

After the Battle of Maysalun, General Gouraud's forces entered Damascus on July 25, 1920. This marked the official beginning of French rule in Syria. The defeat of Faisal's forces and his subsequent exile effectively ended the brief existence of the Arab Kingdom of Syria. Gouraud dissolved the Syrian government and imposed direct French control over the region.

Division of Territories: Gouraud implemented a divide-and-rule strategy to manage the diverse and often fractious populations under French control. He divided Syria and Lebanon into several separate states.

The creation of the states of : Damascus, Aleppo , Alawite, Jabal Greater Lebanon and Alexandretta. Made up the newly divided regions that General Gouraud created.

This division aimed to weaken nationalist movements by fostering regional and sectarian divisions. Gouraud used military force to deal with local uprisings and resistance to French rule. Notable revolts included those led by the Druze and other local groups, met with harsh reprisals.

The French military employed heavy artillery, aerial bombardments, and other severe measures to suppress dissent and control the territories.

Despite the harsh measures, Gouraud also focused on modernizing the infrastructure in the mandate territories. This included building roads, railways, and schools to integrate the region into the French colonial framework.

The French administration sought to exploit the region's resources for financial gain, reinforcing their control through economic dependency.

Gouraud's administration worked closely with the British to maintain mutual interests in the Middle East, including respecting the boundaries established by the Sykes-Picot Agreement.

Gouraud negotiated treaties with local tribal leaders and influential figures to secure their allegiance and cooperation, often using a combination of incentives and threats.

Impact on Regional Politics

Gouraud's policies of division and suppression sowed the seeds of long-term sectarian and regional divisions that have continued to affect Syrian and Lebanese politics.

Rise of Nationalism: Despite efforts to suppress nationalist movements, the harsh measures and division strategies ultimately fueled a more organized and determined nationalist movement in the following decades.

His strategies of military suppression, administrative division, and infrastructure development laid the groundwork for French colonial rule but also contributed to the enduring complexities and conflicts in the region.

The attacks on Jewish settlements in Palestine following the establishment of Syria under the French Mandate were driven by a complex interplay of political, social, and economic factors. These included heightened nationalist sentiments, demographic changes, economic competition, and reactions to external political developments.

Syrian and Palestinian Nationalism: The imposition of the French Mandate in Syria galvanized Arab nationalist sentiments not only in Syria but also in Palestine. Many Arabs in Palestine viewed the Jewish settlements as part of a broader colonial project supported by Western powers, similar to the French and British mandates. The Jewish settlements along Palestine's borders became a target of resentment of Arabs in French controlled regions despite existing in British-held lands.

Tel Hai had become an established settlement in the area of Gaille Palestine. Gangs of former Syrian fighters formed in the border region, seeking French soldiers to fight; Bedouin and Arab militias began to attack the Jewish settlements and villages, and even Arabs were also assaulted by the[1]Bedouins[2]. The French's defeat of the Syrian King served to fuel the anger toward the French and British.

On March 1, more than a hundred Bedouins marched into Tel Hai looking for a fight with French troops but found there were none to defend the border (16)

CHAPTER#5

The beginning of the Jewish military militia.

The early Jewish settlers in Palestine faced significant challenges in defending themselves against Arab invasions, particularly from Syrian Bedouins. Despite generally peaceful relations with their Arab and Christian neighbors—who at times even protected them by offering shelter—the settlers lacked military training and basic weapons like rifles. To address this, the Jewish Agency began supplying the settlers with weapons and organizing self-defense training.

Joseph Trumpeldor, a key figure in the Jewish resistance, played a crucial role in leading these training efforts until his death during an Arab attack on the Tel Hai settlement. Many of the early attacks on Jewish settlements were driven by Arab anger toward the British Mandate and resentment over their defeat by the French in Syria. This rising threat forced the Yishuv (the Jewish community in Palestine) to establish the Haganah, the first organized Zionist defense force, to protect settlements along the borders of Syria and Lebanon. Trumpeldor's initial efforts in training the settlers laid the foundation for this militia. .

The majority of the early attacks were the result of the Arab anger toward the Mandate and the defeat by the French in Syria. (17) These attacks forced the Yishiva to create the first of the Zionist militia's defense forces to protect Jewish villages and settlements on the borders of Syria and Lebanon.

---

1. https://en.wikipedia.org/wiki/Bedouin

2. https://en.wikipedia.org/wiki/Bedouin

They were known as the "[3]Haganah[4],"[5] and Joseph Trumpeldor originally trained the members.

The Yishivia created a group of night patrols and village defenders to fight off these attacks.

As the violence began to spread throughout the border region that affected both Arab and Jewish settlements, The "night patrols" of the Haganah would retaliate against suspect Arab nomads and villages in Palestine.

The Haganah became an offensive militia unit and expanded their actions with patrols and training and supply weapons to attack Arabs, even those that were non-combatants.

One of the most prominent leaders of the Haganah was Ze[6][7]ev[8]Jabotinsky[9], who became active in the Zionist movement in the early 1900s, focusing on Jewish self-defense and promoting Jewish statehood in Palestine.

In response to pogroms in Russia, Jabotinsky organized Jewish self-defense units to protect Jewish communities from violence. During World War I, Jabotinsky proposed creating a Jewish military unit to fight alongside the British against the Ottoman Empire. His efforts led to the formation of the Jewish Legion, composed of battalions within the British Army, including the 38th, 39th, and 40th Battalions of the Royal Fusiliers.

Jabotinsky was a lieutenant in the 38th Battalion of the Jewish Legion. The Jewish Legion fought in the Palestine Campaign, contributing to the British victory.

---

3. https://en.wikipedia.org/wiki/Haganah

4. https://en.wikipedia.org/wiki/Haganah

5. https://en.wikipedia.org/wiki/Haganah

6. https://en.jabotinsky.org/

7. https://en.jabotinsky.org/

8. https://en.jabotinsky.org/

9. https://en.jabotinsky.org/

Ze'ev Jabotsky was a former member of the British military who served in World War 1 with the Zion Mule Corps, which he created with Joseph Trumpeldor.

At the war's end,continued to teach Jews combat methods. He pushed the Yishivia to develop youth self-defense units. He later created the paramilitary groupBetar[10] in Latvia, the youth movementHatzohar[11], and then a militant organization like the terrorist group known as Irgun.

The Arab nationalists in Palestine were reacted to the increase of Jews into the region as immigrants, which they believed threatened their land and the economy of the community, began to call for attacks on Jews in the area. Anti-Zionist speeches followed the[12] 1920 [13]Nebi[14]Musa[15]riot[16], which was one of the most violent riots during this period. The Arab Nationalist speeches catalyzed the transformation of the political landscape. These speeches, characterized by charismatic oratory and emotional calls for unity among Arabs, painted a vivid picture of Arab nationalism.

They spoke of a shared history, a common language, and, most importantly, a collective struggle against perceived injustices. This united front was a powerful tool that could significantly sway public sentiment. The speeches served to ignite a sense of shared identity among the Arabs, fostering a feeling of unity and shared purpose against what they perceived as an encroaching Jewish presence in their lands.

---

10. https://en.wikipedia.org/wiki/Betar

11. https://en.wikipedia.org/wiki/Hatzohar

12. https://en.wikipedia.org/wiki/1920_Nebi_Musa_riots

13. https://en.wikipedia.org/wiki/1920_Nebi_Musa_riots

14. https://en.wikipedia.org/wiki/1920_Nebi_Musa_riots

15. https://en.wikipedia.org/wiki/1920_Nebi_Musa_riots

16. https://en.wikipedia.org/wiki/1920_Nebi_Musa_riots

Arab nationalists began to vocalize their frustrations more intensely, their speeches framed the Jews as invaders and a common enemy encroaching upon Arab territory. This portrayal resonated widely among the Arab population, deepening the wedge between the two communities. The Jews, in turn, became more isolated, and resentment toward them grew, leading to frequent clashes and hostility.

Despite these growing tensions, the British administration made little effort to quell the violence or mediate between the Arabs and Jews. Their apathy toward both sides allowed the situation to spiral out of control. Instead of addressing the root causes of the unrest—such as land disputes, economic inequality, and fears over political dominance—the British remained largely indifferent.

This lack of decisive action not only emboldened Arab nationalists but also marginalized the Jewish community further.

The riots of 1920 were a tragic result of this festering conflict. The British authorities' failure to foresee and prevent the violence, or even to manage it effectively once it erupted, highlighted their broader indifference to the mounting tensions. The growing extremism in Arab rhetoric, combined with Jewish fears of being overrun, created an environment ripe for conflict. And in this atmosphere, the British policy of inaction only exacerbated the underlying issues.

The British played a passive role in a region teetering on the brink of collapse. Their refusal to take firm action to mediate between the Jews and Arabs, coupled with their ineffective governance, contributed to the widening divide between the two groups.

The political landscape of the Middle East was significantly transformed by Arab Nationalist speeches, which heightened tensions between Jewish and Arab communities. These speeches fostered a shared identity among Arabs. They portrayed Jews as a common enemy, culminating in the Nebi Musa riots in 1920. (18)

Chapter #6 The Riots of Palestine Jews and Arabs.

Sir[17]Ronald[18]Henry[19]Amherst[20]Storrs[21],[22] who served as the Military
Governor of Jerusalem within
theOccupied[23]Enemy[24]Territory[25]Administration[26], was approached
by Jabotinsky with a plan to protect Jews following the riots, but his
plan was rejected. The riots of 1920 occurred over several days and
resulted in the injury and deaths of both Jews and Arabs. Jabotinsky
and the[27]Mayor[28]of[29]Jerusalem[30], [31]Musa[32]Kazim[33]Al[34]Husagni[35],[36]
were tried for taking part in the riot and convicted. Jabotsky's home
and office were searched, several of the men he trained started the riot,
and the British military courts convicted and sentenced them to
prison. Jabotinsky claimed that he was their military trainer and

17. https://www.npg.org.uk/collections/search/person/mp06057/sir-ronald-henry-amherst-storrs

18. https://www.npg.org.uk/collections/search/person/mp06057/sir-ronald-henry-amherst-storrs

19. https://www.npg.org.uk/collections/search/person/mp06057/sir-ronald-henry-amherst-storrs

20. https://www.npg.org.uk/collections/search/person/mp06057/sir-ronald-henry-amherst-storrs

21. https://www.npg.org.uk/collections/search/person/mp06057/sir-ronald-henry-amherst-storrs

22. https://www.npg.org.uk/collections/search/person/mp06057/sir-ronald-henry-amherst-storrs

23. https://en.wikipedia.org/wiki/Occupied_Enemy_Territory_Administration

24. https://en.wikipedia.org/wiki/Occupied_Enemy_Territory_Administration

25. https://en.wikipedia.org/wiki/Occupied_Enemy_Territory_Administration

26. https://en.wikipedia.org/wiki/Occupied_Enemy_Territory_Administration

27. https://en.wikipedia.org/wiki/Musa_al-Husayni#Interaction_with_Jews_and_Zionists

28. https://en.wikipedia.org/wiki/Musa_al-Husayni#Interaction_with_Jews_and_Zionists

29. https://en.wikipedia.org/wiki/Musa_al-Husayni#Interaction_with_Jews_and_Zionists

30. https://en.wikipedia.org/wiki/Musa_al-Husayni#Interaction_with_Jews_and_Zionists

31. https://en.wikipedia.org/wiki/Musa_al-Husayni#Interaction_with_Jews_and_Zionists

32. https://en.wikipedia.org/wiki/Musa_al-Husayni#Interaction_with_Jews_and_Zionists

33. https://en.wikipedia.org/wiki/Musa_al-Husayni#Interaction_with_Jews_and_Zionists

34. https://en.wikipedia.org/wiki/Musa_al-Husayni#Interaction_with_Jews_and_Zionists

35. https://en.wikipedia.org/wiki/Musa_al-Husayni#Interaction_with_Jews_and_Zionists

36. https://en.wikipedia.org/wiki/Musa_al-Husayni#Interaction_with_Jews_and_Zionists

Leader and demanded that he also be tried. He was convicted and given a 15-year prison sentence.

The[37]Zionist[38]Revisionist[39]beliefs of Jabotinsky were the basis of his conviction for why the riots occurred. The Revisionists believed that they would never obtain a homeland in Palestine without violence. Weisman and the leaders of the Yeshiva would use Jabotinsky's skills in training for combat in the formation of the Haganah. But they rejected his views on Zionism, that only violent action would cause change in Palestine and create a Jewish state. The riots in 1920 served as proof to the leadership of the Yeshiva and Weisman that an armed paramilitary force like the Haganah was needed to protect the Jews in settlements and attacks that occurred in the cities.

Arab nationalists viewed the creation of the Haganah as a direct threat to their national aspirations and security. The existence of a Jewish paramilitary force was seen as an indication of the Jewish community's intention to defend and possibly expand their settlements at the expense of the Arab population. The formation of the Haganah spurred Arab nationalists to organize their paramilitary groups and intensify their resistance against Jewish settlements. This led to an escalation in violent encounters and contributed to the broader cycle of retaliatory attacks between Jewish and Arab communities.

The British authorities were deeply concerned about the potential for civil war in Palestine, given the increasing militarization of both Jewish and Arab communities. Establishing the Haganah was seen as a destabilizing factor that could lead to widespread violence and undermine British control.

The British administration attempted to maintain order by imposing restrictions on Jewish and Arab paramilitary activities. They sought to

---

37. https://www.jewishvirtuallibrary.org/revisionist-zionism

38. https://www.jewishvirtuallibrary.org/revisionist-zionism

39. https://www.jewishvirtuallibrary.org/revisionist-zionism

prevent the escalation of violence through policing actions, curfews, and other security measures.

This narrative resonated widely among the Arab population, fostering a sense of resentment and hostility toward the Jewish community. The increasingly vitriolic speeches marginalized the Jewish community further, amplifying the tension between the two groups. The Arab Nationalist speeches catalyzed a transformative shift in the political landscape.

These speeches, marked by charismatic oratory and impassioned calls for unity among Arabs, painted a vivid tableau of Arab nationalism.

The implementation of the British Mandate for Palestine in 1922 added fuel to the already simmering resentment among the Arabs. The Mandate, while facilitating Jewish immigration, denied the native Arab population any significant control over their land or governance. It effectively limited the rights of the Arabs while favoring the Jewish immigrants, leading to further discontent and resentment among the Arab population. The Arabs viewed the Mandate as a continuation of the injustices started by the Balfour Declaration, exacerbating the rise of Arab nationalism.

These sentiments were further inflamed by the Balfour Declaration and the British Mandate for Palestine, which were perceived as blatant foreign interventions in Arab affairs. The Balfour Declaration, in particular, was seen as a significant betrayal, promising a 'national home for the Jewish people' in Palestine, a land that Arabs considered their own.

The rise of Arab nationalism also led to increased polarization, with both communities increasingly viewing each other as enemies rather than fellow inhabitants of the same land. In response to rising tensions and violent confrontations with Arab communities, the Haganah began to adopt a more aggressive stance. The Haganah also emerged as a threat to the British military in Palestine. The group's growing strength and assertiveness, coupled with its opposition to British policies, led to confrontations with British forces, further escalating the complex political situation in Palestine.

On May 2, Jews in theHaganah[40] began launching reprisal attacks on Arabs, "[41]the[42]Jaffa[43]riot[44],"[45] the first of their kind. Armed with automatic weapons, at least one group of Haganah militants broke into Arab homes with instructions to "destroy everything." The chief force behind the creation of the Haganah,Eliyahu[46]Golomb[47], reported that at least one of the group's militants had killed a disabled Arab and his children in an orange grove. Several Jews were arrested, including one policeman, for their suspected involvement in the shooting of Arab civilians. Still, they were not charged due to lack of evidence. . Of the 48 Arab dead, mostly killed by the British police force, it was unclear how many were killed in revenge attacks by Jews. The initial reaction among the Arab population in Palestine to the Balfour Declaration and the Sykes-Picot Agreement was one of disbelief and a profound sense of betrayal. Many Arabs had been led to believe that their support for the Allies during World War I would

---

40. https://en.wikipedia.org/wiki/Haganah

41. https://www.timesofisrael.com/1921-jaffa-riots-100-years-on-mandatory-palestines-1st-mass-casualty-event/

42. https://www.timesofisrael.com/1921-jaffa-riots-100-years-on-mandatory-palestines-1st-mass-casualty-event/

43. https://www.timesofisrael.com/1921-jaffa-riots-100-years-on-mandatory-palestines-1st-mass-casualty-event/

44. https://www.timesofisrael.com/1921-jaffa-riots-100-years-on-mandatory-palestines-1st-mass-casualty-event/

45. https://www.timesofisrael.com/1921-jaffa-riots-100-years-on-mandatory-palestines-1st-mass-casualty-event/

46. https://en.wikipedia.org/wiki/Eliyahu_Golomb

47. https://en.wikipedia.org/wiki/Eliyahu_Golomb

establish independent Arab states, as implied by the correspondence between Sharif Hussein of Mecca and Sir Henry McMahon.(13)

As the implications of the Balfour Declaration became clearer, opposition grew. Arab leaders and intellectuals organized protests and articulated their grievances, emphasizing the incompatibility of the establishment of a Jewish national home with the political and national aspirations of the Arab majority in Palestine.

Britain's reactions to the Balfour Declaration and the Sykes-Picot Agreement were mixed. While the government and many political leaders supported the establishment of a Jewish national home, there was significant debate and opposition within political and public circles.

Critics of the Balfour Declaration, including some British politicians and public figures, argued that it contradicted promises made to the Arabs and would lead to instability and conflict. Prominent figures such as Edwin[48]Montagu[49], the Secretary of State for India, expressed concern that the declaration would foster anti-Semitism and jeopardize British interests in the Middle East.

The growing conflict in Palestine and the broader Middle East challenged British strategic interests, particularly regarding access to oil resources and maintaining stability in the region. The British government had to navigate the competing demands of Zionist and Arab nationalist movements while safeguarding its economic interests.

High[50]Commissioner[51]Herbert[52]Samuel[53] declared a state of emergency and imposed press censorship in response to rising tensions

---

48. https://www.britannica.com/biography/Edwin-Samuel-Montagu

49. https://www.britannica.com/biography/Edwin-Samuel-Montagu

50. https://en.wikipedia.org/wiki/Herbert_Samuel,_1st_Viscount_Samuel

51. https://en.wikipedia.org/wiki/Herbert_Samuel,_1st_Viscount_Samuel

52. https://en.wikipedia.org/wiki/Herbert_Samuel,_1st_Viscount_Samuel

between Jews and Arabs. The British Army was called upon to send reinforcements from Egypt, and General Allenby dispatched two ships, one to Haifa and one to Jaffa, carrying armed troops.

The conflict quickly spread beyond the major cities to smaller communities, including Rehovot, Kfar Saba, Petah Tikva, and Hadera, where fighting continued for several days. British aircraft even dropped bombs to "protect Jewish settlements from Arab raiders." Both sides engaged in retaliatory attacks, escalating the violence. In response, High Commissioner Samuel established an investigative commission, led by the Chief Justice of the Supreme Court in Palestine, Sir[54] Thomas[55] Haycraft[56], to examine the causes of the unrest. Leaders of the Revisionist Zionist movement, such as Ze'ev Jabotinsky and David Raziel, concluded that armed resistance was the only effective way to protect Jews in Palestine. They believed the Yishuv's traditional approach of cooperation with the British authorities was insufficient in the face of attacks from both local Arabs and raiders from Syria. As a result, they advocated for a more militant defense strategy.

Efforts by the British to foster cooperation among Jews, Arabs, and their own military officers in the region failed to gain the trust of either side. The Yishuv leadership remained hopeful that the British would continue to support the Balfour Declaration by encouraging Jewish immigration and defending settlements from Arab attacks. The Jewish defense organization Haganah began organizing patrols and establishing units in each settlement to fend off nighttime raids. Meanwhile, Arab nationalist leaders accused these Jewish defense units of carrying out offensive attacks against them, and they too sought protection from the British military.

---

53. https://en.wikipedia.org/wiki/Herbert_Samuel,_1st_Viscount_Samuel

54. https://balfourproject.org/the-report-of-the-haycraft-commission-of-inquiry-1921/

55. https://balfourproject.org/the-report-of-the-haycraft-commission-of-inquiry-1921/

56. https://balfourproject.org/the-report-of-the-haycraft-commission-of-inquiry-1921/

By 1929, tensions between Arabs and Jews had reached a new height, particularly over conflicting claims to the Western Wall (referred to as the "Wailing Wall"). Both communities intensified their propaganda efforts, further deepening the divide.

The 1929 Riot August 23-29.

Joseph[57]Klausner[58], a prominent scholar and far-right Leader, played a crucial role in

the events leading to the 1929 riots. (19) Klausner, an ardent Zionist, was closely

associated with the Revisionist Zionist movement, Ze'ev Jabotinsky. The Revisionist Zionists was also known for his nationalist fervor and the goal of

establishing a Jewish state on both sides of the Jordan River. Klausner's fiery

speeches and protest marches aimed at asserting Jewish rights to the Western

Wall was instrumental in setting off a chain of events that led to the riots.

The 1929 riots were marked by a high degree of violence and resulted in

significant loss of life and property. The Jewish communities in Hebron and Safed

were particularly hard hit, with scores of Jews being killed and many others being

forced to flee their homes. The riots marked a significant escalation in Jewish-

Arab tensions.

"[59]The[60]Shaw[61]Commission[62]"[63]

---

57. https://en.wikipedia.org/wiki/Joseph_Klausner

58. https://en.wikipedia.org/wiki/Joseph_Klausner

59. https://en.wikipedia.org/wiki/Shaw_Commission

60. https://en.wikipedia.org/wiki/Shaw_Commission

The Shaw commission was appointed to investigate the riots,
attributed the violence to Arab fears of
increasing Jewish immigration and the perceived threat to Muslim
holy places. (20)
The report led to the issuance of the[64]Passfield[65]White[66]Paper[67],[68]
which recommended
limiting Jewish immigration and land purchases, a move that
provoked widespread
opposition among the Zionists.
Arab Nationalist speeches significantly altered the Middle East's
political landscape, heightening
tensions between Jewish and Arab communities and leading to the
Nebi Musa
riots in 1920. The riots that began in 1920 persisted for a month
without resolution. The aftermath of the 1920 riots extended for a
decade with attacks on villages and settlements of both Arabs and Jews
without any actual effort to resolve the conflict by the British
government for the next decade.
In 1929, there was an attack on the city of Hebron in Palestine, which
had a population of around 20,000 people, the majority of whom were
Arabs. The attack was the result of escalating violence between Jews
and Arabs.
At the time, there were rumors in the Arab community that Jews were
planning an attack on the Temple Mount in Jerusalem, which led to

61. https://en.wikipedia.org/wiki/Shaw_Commission

62. https://en.wikipedia.org/wiki/Shaw_Commission

63. https://en.wikipedia.org/wiki/Shaw_Commission

64. https://www.jewishvirtuallibrary.org/jsource/History/passfield.html,

65. https://www.jewishvirtuallibrary.org/jsource/History/passfield.html,

66. https://www.jewishvirtuallibrary.org/jsource/History/passfield.html,

67. https://www.jewishvirtuallibrary.org/jsource/History/passfield.html,

68. https://www.jewishvirtuallibrary.org/jsource/History/passfield.html,

further animosity between the two groups. Although Jews in Hebron had not previously been targeted like other communities, they were not spared during the attack.

The[69]Safed[70]Massacre[71]on[72]August[73] 29, 1929[74], was a tragic event rooted in escalating tensions between Jews and Arabs in Palestine during the British Mandate period. Several key factors contributed to the outbreak of violence in Safed, a city with a significant history of Jewish-Arab coexistence but also underlying tensions. Both Jewish and Arab communities in Palestine were becoming increasingly nationalistic. The Zionist movement's efforts to establish a Jewish homeland in Palestine were met with growing resistance from the Arab population of the city who feared displacement and loss of their land and political dominance.

The violence led to increased militarization of both Jewish and Arab communities. The Haganah, the Jewish defense organization, expanded its activities to protect Jewish settlements. The events further polarized the Jewish and Arab communities and solidified mutual distrust. It also influenced British policies, leading to the issuance of the Passfield White Paper in 1930, which attempted to limit Jewish immigration and land purchases. However, it was met with opposition from both communities.

The 1930s in Palestine were marked for both Jews and Muslim Arabs of divisions in nationalism. Amin al-Husseini faced radical opposition to his leadership of Palestinian people from a clandestine group

---

69. https://en.wikipedia.org/wiki/1929_Palestine_riots#CITEREFShaw_Commission1930

70. https://en.wikipedia.org/wiki/1929_Palestine_riots#CITEREFShaw_Commission1930

71. https://en.wikipedia.org/wiki/1929_Palestine_riots#CITEREFShaw_Commission1930

72. https://en.wikipedia.org/wiki/1929_Palestine_riots#CITEREFShaw_Commission1930

73. https://en.wikipedia.org/wiki/1929_Palestine_riots#CITEREFShaw_Commission1930

74. https://en.wikipedia.org/wiki/1929_Palestine_riots#CITEREFShaw_Commission1930

known as the "[75]Black[76]Hand[77]"[78] created by Izz Ad-Qassam, who was appointed as the imam of a mosque in Haifa by Husseini. (21)

In the past, the "Black Hand" called for a Jihad against the Jews and the British. His group targeted their attacks on Jewish settlements, small groups of Jewish homes, and anyone who supported Zionism, including Druze and Christian Arabs. This caused a split between his group and Husseini.

The widespread violence and the perceived bias of the British administration towards Jewish immigrants greatly influenced Al-Qassam's ideology. He regarded the riots as a clear demonstration of the failure of peaceful resistance and began advocating for armed struggle.

The 1929 riots catalyzed the "Black Hand" formation and subsequent activities, but the group could not take control over the majority of Arab Palestinians.In the past, the "Black Hand" called for a Jihad against the Jews and the British. His group targeted their attacks on Jewish settlements, small groups of Jewish homes, and anyone who supported Zionism, including Druze and Christian Arabs.

.

The British military provided the Haganah with extensive training, weapons, and authority to attack Muslim Arabs in rural areas and arrest suspects in cities. As punishment for hiding or withholding information from the military or police, the suspects' homes were destroyed.

British authorities viewed the Haganah with suspicion but allowed it to exist as a self-defense force. In the early 1930s, tensions between Arab and Jewish communities in Palestine increased, fueled by political, economic, and social factors. As tensions rose, protests and

---

75. https://en.wikipedia.org/wiki/Black_Hand_(Serbia)

76. https://en.wikipedia.org/wiki/Black_Hand_(Serbia)

77. https://en.wikipedia.org/wiki/Black_Hand_(Serbia)

78. https://en.wikipedia.org/wiki/Black_Hand_(Serbia)

strikes against British rule led to repressive measures by the British authorities.

The 1929 riots were a crucial moment in the Jewish-Arab conflict. The widespread violence and perceived bias of the British towards Jewish immigrants profoundly influenced Al-Qassam's views. He saw the riots as evidence that peaceful resistance had failed and began advocating for armed struggle. The 1929 riots led to the formation of the "Black Hand," but the goal of the group was to gain control over the Nationalist movement which it failed to do. The Black Hand had 200 to 600 men and attacked Jewish settlements in Northern Palestine using small cells of fighters and from 1930 to 1935 . The group was never supported by the Nationalist movement and on November 30 1935 following the attack and murder of a British policeman the British police forces caught Al Qassam hiding in a cave and killed him. His name became the symbol of armed resistance in the middle east.

Chapter #7 The Arab Nationalist Revolt (1936-1939)

The Arab Nationalist Revolt of 1936-1939, also known as the Great Arab Revolt, was a significant uprising against British colonial rule and Jewish immigration in Palestine. (22)

Arrests:

In response to acts of civil disobedience, including strikes and protests, the British authorities employed a strategy of arrests to quell dissent. Political leaders, activists, and individuals involved in organizing or participating in demonstrations were often targeted. The goal was to disrupt the leadership of the protest movements and discourage further participation.

The imposition of curfews was another standard repressive measure used by the British authorities. Curfews were enforced to restrict the movement of the population during specific hours, limiting their ability to gather, organize, or participate in protests. This tactic aimed to control the situation and prevent the escalation of unrest.

The British Mandate government also employed force to suppress dissent. This included the deployment of military and police forces to disperse crowds, break up protests, and maintain order. The use of force sometimes resulted in clashes between demonstrators and security forces, leading to injuries and fatalities.

The British authorities implemented measures to restrict political activities that were perceived as a threat to their control. This involved suppressing political organizations, limiting freedom of assembly, and monitoring the activities of political leaders. Such restrictions aimed to stifle the organizational capacity of dissenting groups.

Censorship was another tool used by the British authorities to control the narrative and prevent the spread of information that could incite further unrest. Publications and communication channels were closely monitored, and content deemed subversive or inflammatory was often censored.

The British Police expanded their numbers in Palestine from 900- to 2500 and began creating police departments called Taggart Forts, named after their designer,Irish[79] police officer and engineerSir[80]Charles[81]Tegart[82]. The design was to prevent prolonged attacks and serve as prisons with few exits. The upper wall allowed for above-ground firing on attempts to scale the walls.

The years 1930 to 36 revealed that with the Mandate, the British and French were vulnerable to economic uprisings as strikes, and the 1931 strike led to independence in Iraq. The strike had far-reaching implications, both domestically and within Syria. It galvanized the Syrian population, fostering a sense of unity and national identity that transcended regional, sectarian, and class boundaries. Internationally, it drew global attention to the Syrian struggle, highlighting the harsh

---

79. https://en.wikipedia.org/wiki/Irish_people

80. https://en.wikipedia.org/wiki/Charles_Tegart

81. https://en.wikipedia.org/wiki/Charles_Tegart

82. https://en.wikipedia.org/wiki/Charles_Tegart

realities of French colonial rule and generating sympathy for the Syrian cause. The strike's impact was so profound that it forced the French authorities to enter into negotiations withthe[83]Syrian[84]National[85]Movement[86].
However, the British continued in Palestine to increase policing and make arrests.

.

The British were forced to in Palestine increase the amount of patrol for attacks on railroads, oil pipelines, and settlements. The Yishuv, working with the Haganah, created with Ze'ev Jobotinsky, the far-right group Irgun (created in 1931), as a Jewish paramilitary group. The Irgun was designed to launch terrorist attacks on the Muslim Arabs. Jobotinsky believed that retaliation would deter the Arabs. (23)
The British military allowed many of its officers, who supported the Zionist movement, to train Jews who volunteered to fight against the Revolt.

Orde[87]Charles[88]Wingate[89] was a British Army officer who became known for his support of the Zionist cause in British Mandatory Palestine during the 1930s. He proposed and created the Special Night Squads (SNS), composed of British soldiers and Jewish volunteers. (24)The SNS's objective was to conduct raids against Arab insurgents during the Arab Rebellion of 1936-1939. Wingate's methods included unconventional guerrilla tactics.

---

83. https://en.wikipedia.org/wiki/Syrian_nationalism

84. https://en.wikipedia.org/wiki/Syrian_nationalism

85. https://en.wikipedia.org/wiki/Syrian_nationalism

86. https://en.wikipedia.org/wiki/Syrian_nationalism

87. https://war-experience.org/lives/major-general-orde-wingate-1903-1944/

88. https://war-experience.org/lives/major-general-orde-wingate-1903-1944/

89. https://war-experience.org/lives/major-general-orde-wingate-1903-1944/

Wingate's influence on the Zionist Jews under his command had several dimensions: Special Night Squads (SNSs): Wingate established the SNSs, which were small, mobile units designed to carry out surprise nighttime raids on rebel positions and villages suspected of aiding the enemy. These squads were composed of British soldiers and Jewish volunteers who operated under the cover of darkness to leverage the element of surprise and combat the insurgents' guerrilla warfare with their version. The idea was to use the tactics of the rebels against them. Night operations were especially a marked departure from conventional military practices. These tactics would later become part of the development of Israeli army strategies.

The Irgun terrorist group had a larger plan by Ze'ev Jabotinsky, the Leader of the Revisionist Zionist movement, to overthrow the British in Palestine with a revolt in October 1939. They would seize power over Palestine while Zionist supporters in Europe and America would declare that Israel was a nation in exile. (25)Avraham Stern also created a plan that would bring 40,000 Jewish fighters to Palestine to fight the British and force the Muslim Arabs to leave Palestine. The Polish government supported his plan and began to make plans for the attack by training Jewish fighters. Still, on September 1, 1939, World War Two began. The leadership of Irgun suspended its actions against the British military and police. Jabotinsky redirected the militia members to join the Haganah and the British Army. Avraham[90]Stern[91],[92] the Leader of the Lehi (Stern gang), refused to support the British and created a new militia known as "Lehi." The original name was the National Military Organization in Israel, but it became Lehi. (24) It was a far-right Revisionist organized by Stern that planned on continuing to fight the British military even though the Jewish leadership of the Jewish Agency for Palestine questioned

---

90. https://www.jewishvirtuallibrary.org/avraham-stern

91. https://www.jewishvirtuallibrary.org/avraham-stern

92. https://www.jewishvirtuallibrary.org/avraham-stern

the need for the group., David Ben-Gurion, directed Jewish men to join the British Army to fight against the Nazi forces at the beginning of the second world war.

Lehi found that the British support of the White Paper and the Mandate was a more significant threat to the creation of a Jewish state in Palestine by limiting immigration and forcing and blocking attempts by Jews to enter the country, a more significant threat to Jewish lives and a reason for the creation of the concentration camps. The influence that Stern had over the members of Lehi caused the group to be known as the "Stern Gang." The Stern gang committed terrorist acts against the British government and acts of violence against Arabs.

In December 1940, Lehi contacted Germany with a proposal to aid the German conquest in the Middle East in return for recognition of a Jewish state open to unlimited immigration. Still, the Nazis failed to accept his proposal.

On January 11, 1941, Vice Admiral Ralf von der Marwitz, the German navalattaché[93] in Turkey[94], filed a report (the "Ankara document") conveying Lehi's offer to "actively take part in the war on Germany's side" in return for German support for "the establishment of the historical Jewish state on a national and totalitarian basis, bound by a treaty with the German Reich. (25)

Lehi's unusual stance of viewing Britain as a greater adversary than Hitler, despite the full scale of Nazi atrocities becoming evident, was a significant divergence from the majority view during World War II. Rooted in their belief that the British were the primary obstacle to Jewish statehood in Palestine, this view shaped Lehi's actions and had far-reaching consequences, both within Palestine and in the broader context of the Zionist movement. Despite acknowledging the horrors

---

93. https://en.wikipedia.org/wiki/Attach%C3%A9

94. https://en.wikipedia.org/wiki/Turkey

being perpetrated by the Nazis, Lehi did not see Hitler and Nazi Germany as the main enemy.

They continued to focus their antagonism towards the British Mandate authorities in Palestine They argued that the British policy of limiting Jewish immigration, especially against the backdrop of the Holocaust, was a significant betrayal. Moreover, they believed that the British favored the Arab population and were unwilling to act against Arab aggression toward Jews. Lehi's stance led to a series of actions fundamentally different from other Jewish and Zionist organizations of the time. They launched attacks against the British authorities in Palestine, including assassinations of high-ranking officials. These activities isolated Lehi from the mainstream Jewish leadership and populace, who were more focused on the plight of European Jewry and the fight against Hitler.

Lehi's stance had significant consequences. On one hand, it increased the tension between the Jewish community and the British administration in Palestine. On the other hand, it also led to divisions within the Zionist movement, as Lehi's activities and consequences were not universally accepted.

The founder of the Lehi, Avraham Stern, and Avraham Tehomi, had received their training through the Haganah, and both served in Irgrun. Still, they became unhappy with the Yishiva regarding the British and fought them over immigration. Stern was in Palestine when the Second World War began and at the time and was arrested the same night the war started. He was incarcerated together with the entire High Command of the Irgun in the Jerusalem Central Prison and Sarafand Detention Camp.

Once he was released, he formed the Lehi, but they had few members and no funding for weapons. The Jewish Authority refused to support their actions unless they approved it first.

The members of Lehi resorted to extortion and even bank robberies to obtain the money they needed. The group attacked British police stations
railroads and shopping areas, and *Assassinated* those who opposed their form of Zionism.
The robberies resulted in the death of Jews caught in the crossfire between his men and the police. Stern viewed this as a part of the Zionist
relationship to obtain a Jewish homeland, but the Lehi leader saw that any action against the British government that assisted in immigration, even the assassination of other Jews that rejected their cause, was acceptable.
Avraham Stern and the members of Lehi developed a plan to work with the Nazis and Italians to attack the British during the second world war as a trade for Jewish immigration to Palestine.
But their plan was never accepted by the Nazis or Italians. The British intelligence and Irgrun became aware of their activities. The plan failed, and Stern was exposed. He became one of the most wanted terrorists in Palestine by the British police, and he was hunted down, captured, and killed by the Mandate police.
Lehi's stance led to a series of actions fundamentally different from other Jewish and Zionist organizations of the time. They launched attacks against the British authorities in Palestine, including assassinations of high-ranking officials. These activities isolated Lehi from the mainstream Jewish leadership and populace, who were more focused on the plight of European Jewry and the fight against Hitler.
Furthermore, Lehi's stance had significant consequences. On the one hand, it increased the tension between the Jewish community and the British administration in Palestine.
This also led to divisions within the Zionist movement, as Lehi's activities and consequences were not universally accepted. Lehi's unusual stance of viewing Britain as a greater adversary than Hitler,

despite the full scale of Nazi atrocities becoming evident, Rooted in their belief that the British were the primary obstacle to Jewish statehood in Palestine,

The Jewish community was encouraged to join the British Army by the Jewish Agency and the Yeshiva in Palestine. Thousands of Jews joined British Army during WWII despite the immigration controls imposed by the Mandate. The Jewish Agency did not support Lehi's actions against the British but instead encouraged Jews to join and reject Lehi's view that the Nazi would support them if they fought the British.

The Jewish Brigade Group faced issues with discipline and leadership despite being composed of both Jewish and Muslim Arab soldiers.

(26)

The Palestine Regiment was formed in 1942 during the height of World War II, as part of the British Army's efforts to bolster its forces in the Middle East. This new military formation was primarily composed of infantry companies from the Palestine Infantry Companies, which had been attached to the Buffs (Royal East Kent Regiment). The regiment was a unique entity, as it reflected the complex demographic makeup of Mandatory Palestine by including separate Jewish and Arab battalions. The formation of the Palestine Regiment was part of a broader British strategy to involve local populations in the defense of the Middle East, a critical region during the war, given its proximity to key Allied supply routes and its strategic importance in countering Axis powers in North Africa. The regiment was composed of conscripts drawn from both the Jewish and Arab populations of Mandatory Palestine, a decision that mirrored the complex and often tense political landscape of the time. British authorities had hoped that by integrating both communities into a single regiment, they could foster cooperation between Jews and Arabs in the region. However, the separation of the regiment into distinct Jewish and Arab battalions indicated the underlying divisions that existed between the two groups, both of which had differing national aspirations for the future of Palestine.

In 1944, the Palestine Regiment underwent reformation, with changes in its structure and deployment as the war progressed. By this time, the regiment had already established a legacy of service, though its role in World War II remained largely defined by guard duties and limited combat engagements. The experience of serving in the regiment, however, was significant for many of its members, as it provided them with military training and an understanding of warfare, experiences that would later shape the future military and political dynamics of the region, particularly as tensions between Jewish and Arab communities continued to grow in the post-war years.

The Formation of Tilhas Tizig Gesheften: A Jewish Response to Nazi atrocities as World War II came to an end and the full horrors of the Holocaust were revealed, a group of Jewish survivors made a historic decision. They formed an organization known as "Tilhas[95]Tizig[96]Gesheften[97]" ([98]TTG[99])[100], which roughly translates to

---

95. https://books.google.com/

books?id=kEs4QwAACAAJ&q=The+Jewish+Brigade:+An+Army+With+Two+Masters,+1944-45.

96. https://books.google.com/

books?id=kEs4QwAACAAJ&q=The+Jewish+Brigade:+An+Army+With+Two+Masters,+1944-45.

97. https://books.google.com/

books?id=kEs4QwAACAAJ&q=The+Jewish+Brigade:+An+Army+With+Two+Masters,+1944-45.

98. https://books.google.com/

books?id=kEs4QwAACAAJ&q=The+Jewish+Brigade:+An+Army+With+Two+Masters,+1944-45.

99. https://books.google.com/

books?id=kEs4QwAACAAJ&q=The+Jewish+Brigade:+An+Army+With+Two+Masters,+1944-45.

"Up to mischief." It was created with a singular purpose in mind: to hunt down Nazis who were responsible for the mass extermination of Jews during the Holocaust. The motivation behind the formation of TTG was a potent mix of revenge, justice, and a desire to prevent the recurrence of such atrocities. The members of TTG were survivors of concentration camps, ghettos, and Nazi-occupied territories. They had witnessed firsthand the brutalities inflicted upon their people. Many had lost their families, friends, and loved ones to the Nazi regime. When the war was over, they were determined to ensure that those responsible for these atrocities were brought to justice. However, the task was not easy.

Many Nazis, anticipating defeat as the war neared its end, had gone into hiding or assumed new identities. Some had fled to countries where they believed they would be safe from prosecution. Tracking them down required resources, skills, and, most importantly, unwavering determination. The TTG, driven by their cause, embarked on this challenging mission. They gathered information, followed leads, and undertook dangerous missions to hunt down Nazis. Their methods were often controversial. They acted outside official legal systems, and their operations involved significant risks. However, for the members of TTG, these risks were justified by their quest for justice. The formation of the Tilhas Tizig Gesheften was a direct response to the horrors of the Holocaust. It was a manifestation of the survivors' resolve to seek justice for their people and to ensure that those responsible for their suffering were held accountable.

The formation of Tilhas Tizig Gesheften (TTG) in the aftermath of World War II marked a significant chapter in the pursuit of justice for Holocaust victims. TTG, composed primarily of Holocaust survivors, dedicated themselves to identifying, locating, and punishing Nazis

---

100. https://books.google.com/

    books?id=kEs4QwAACAAJ&q=The+Jewish+Brigade:+An+Army+With+Two+Masters,+19

    44-45.

and Italians who had perpetrated or contributed to the atrocities of the Holocaust. Their approach markedly differed from the conventional legal avenues of justice, employing methods that could be described as vigilante justice. This unconventional approach significantly impacted the individuals targeted by TTG and broader notions of post-war justice and accountability.

One immediate and tangible impact of TTG's activities was the direct action taken against former Nazis and Italians. Many of these individuals had evaded the initial wave of prosecutions in the immediate post-war period, disappearing into obscurity or assimilating into new communities under assumed identities. TTG's efforts brought many of these individuals out of the shadows, delivering a form of justice that official channels had failed to provide. The vigilante-style operations executed by TTG also served as a stark reminder of the personal and collective trauma suffered by the Jewish community during the Holocaust. TTG's actions were driven by a deep-rooted desire for revenge and justice, a sentiment that resonated strongly with many other survivors and their families. This underscored the lasting psychological impact of the Holocaust and the desperation of its victims to see their tormentors held accountable. On a broader level, TTG's operations sparked a significant debate about the nature of justice and the lengths victims should go to seek it. Some argued that the group's vigilantism undermined the rule of law and the principles of due process of law. The leadership of TTG became a part of Igrun, the Stern gang, and the Haganah after they returned to Palestine, where the British military and the enforcement of the Mandate's "The White Paper" was seen as the cause of the number of deaths during the Holocaust. The Jewish soldiers felt betrayed by the Allied forces after they supported the war against the Axis powers. In 1944, the Palestine Regiment underwent reformation, with changes in its structure and deployment as the war progressed. By this time, the regiment had already established a legacy of service, though its role in

World War II remained largely defined by guard duties and limited combat engagements. The experience of serving in the regiment, however, was significant for many of its members, as it provided them with military training and an understanding of warfare, experiences that would later shape the future military and political dynamics of the region, particularly as tensions between Jewish and Arab communities continued to grow in the post-war years.

Chapter #8 The beginning of the revolt in Palestine .

The British government and the United Nations, following World War 2, continued to enforce the Mandate's White Paper policy. They planned on the creation of a Palestinian Arab state with the Jews as a minority. They believed in the Holocaust survivors becoming a part of Europe and not Palestine. They wanted to protect Britain's position in the Middle Eastern nations.

The Jewish Agency and the Yishiva connected to groups in Europe to begin illegal immigration to Palestine. The British intelligence of MI6 found ships that were planned to be used for illegal immigration. It blew them up in Italy before they could be used. The British Navy created a naval blockade, and the Royal Marines boarded the immigrant ships and forced them to turn back.

This only increased the dissent between the British and the Jews in Palestine. The Atlit detainee camp was opened, and those illegal immigrants who entered Palestine and were captured were held there by the British military.

They also created a detainee location in Cyprus to hold the overflow of illegal immigrants. President Truman formed The Anglo-American

Committee of Inquiry, ajoint[101]British[102]and[103]American[104] committee assembled in Washington, D.C., on January 4, 1946.

The Committee was able to have the British agree to allow 100,000 Jews to immigrate to Palestine. Still, the government did not believe the Muslim Arabs and Jews would accept the rulings of the Committee.

In October of 1945,

Palestine was under the heavy grip of the British Mandate, its future hanging in the balance. The air was filled with anxious anticipation. The resistance, once a scattered collection of groups, was now merging into a united front. The merging of two prominent Jewish paramilitary organizations, the Irgun and the Stern Gang, was about to set the stage for a systemic shift in the struggle against British rule. The Irgun, known for their daring operations and relentless pursuit of an independent Jewish state, were on one side of this merger. The Stern Gang, on the other hand, held a reputation for their radical and uncompromising stance against British rule. Although diverging in certain aspects, their ideologies were united by a shared goal: to end British rule and establish a Jewish state.

The merger of these two forces took time and effort. It was a calculated move borne out of strategic necessity. Both groups recognized that a united front would be far more effective in their struggle against British occupation. Their unity was a potent symbol of resistance that inspired many Jews in Palestine and beyond. The merger marked a critical turning point in the narrative of the Jewish resistance, amplifying the intensity and frequency of their operations. The first signs of a united resistance emerged by September 1945, just a few months after the merger. The newly formed underground

---

101. https://en.wikipedia.org/wiki/United_Kingdom%E2%80%93United_States_relations

102. https://en.wikipedia.org/wiki/United_Kingdom%E2%80%93United_States_relations

103. https://en.wikipedia.org/wiki/United_Kingdom%E2%80%93United_States_relations

104. https://en.wikipedia.org/wiki/United_Kingdom%E2%80%93United_States_relations

organization launched an audacious attack on the British police headquarters in Jerusalem, marking a significant escalation in their campaign against British rule. (27)

Sent shockwaves through the British administration, serving as a stark reminder of the growing strength and audacity of the resistance. The frequency of attacks continued to surge. Railroad tracks were bombed, bridges were blown up, and British military installations were targeted.

The resistance was no longer a sporadic irritant but a formidable force threatening British control over Palestine.

The dawn of 1946 brought with it an escalation not just in the number of attacks but also in their scale and audacity.

The[105] King[106] David[107] Hotel[108] bombing[109] in July, orchestrated by the United Resistance, was a testament to this. The hotel, which hosted the British administrative and military headquarters, was targeted in a brazen daytime attack. The explosion claimed the lives of 91 people, shaking the British administration to its core. (28) The violence only escalated as the year wore on. By December 1946, barely a day passed without news of a new attack against British targets. The frequency and intensity of these attacks indicate the strength and determination of the united resistance. The year 1947 was no different. The resistance continued their relentless campaign against British rule, with attacks becoming increasingly daring and destructive. The British, despite their attempts to quell the violence, found themselves increasingly powerless against the united front of the Irgun and the Stern Gang. Thus, the merger of the Irgun and the Stern Gang ignited a wave of resistance that gradually moved Palestine closer to a revolt against

---

105. https://archive.org/details/jerusalembesiege00eric

106. https://archive.org/details/jerusalembesiege00eric

107. https://archive.org/details/jerusalembesiege00eric

108. https://archive.org/details/jerusalembesiege00eric

109. https://archive.org/details/jerusalembesiege00eric

British rule. The increasing frequency and scale of violent attacks were a testament to the growing strength and determination of the resistance. While the end of this tumultuous chapter was not yet in sight, the events set in motion by the merger were instrumental in shaping the future of Palestine.

U.S. President Truman created the Anglo-American Committee of Inquiry

To work with the British government to increase the number of immigrants to Palestine. The goal was 100,000 and to lower the rate of deported Holocaust survivors back to Europe.

The Contrasting Policies on Palestine: Britain's Mandate and U.S. Immigration Advocacy

During World War II and its immediate aftermath, Britain and the United States, despite being wartime allies, held contrasting stances on the issue of Jewish immigration to Palestine. While the U.S. advocated for an increase in immigration, Britain was determined to maintain its Mandate policies that sought to limit Jewish immigration.

Britain's Determination to Maintain Mandate Policies Britain's determination to maintain its Mandate policies on Palestine was driven by a complex mix of political, strategic, and demographic considerations. Britain was acutely aware of the strategic importance of the Middle East, particularly given its oil resources and geopolitical significance as a link between Europe, Asia, and Africa. Maintaining good relations with the Arab states was critical to securing Britain's regional strategic interests. Secondly, the British authorities dealt with a delicate demographic balance in Palestine. They feared that a significant increase in Jewish immigration would exacerbate tensions with the Arab population, potentially leading to civil unrest and jeopardizing the stability of the region. Britain was also mindful of its international obligations under the League of Nations Mandate.

The Mandate required Britain to prepare Palestine for future self-government. Still, it also called for respecting the civil and religious rights of all inhabitants of Palestine, both Jewish and non-Jewish.

In contrast to Britain, the U.S. was advocating for an increase in Jewish immigration to Palestine. Several factors drove this stance. Firstly, the U.S. was deeply moved by the plight of the Jews in Europe, particularly in the aftermath of the Holocaust. There was a solid moral and humanitarian impetus to provide a refuge for the survivors. Secondly, the U.S. was also influenced by the solid and organized Jewish lobby within its borders. The American Jewish community, deeply affected by the horrors of the Holocaust, was actively advocating for increased Jewish immigration to Palestine.

Thirdly, the U.S. did not share Britain's colonial legacy and associated obligations in the Middle East. This allowed the U.S. to adopt a more flexible and humanitarian stance on the issue of Jewish immigration.

This divergence between two wartime allies underscores the complexity of the Palestine issue and its deep entanglement with broader international politics. President Truman's support for the establishment of a Jewish state in Palestine likely emboldened the Zionist leadership to continue their illegal immigration activities. His endorsement of a Jewish state signaled to the Zionist leaders that they had significant international backing for their cause, potentially making them more willing to defy British immigration restrictions. This support from a considerable world power like the United States also likely boosted morale among the Jewish immigrants and the organizations facilitating their journey to Palestine. Furthermore, U.S. support could have indirectly pressured the British authorities, making it more difficult for them to enforce their immigration policies.

World War II was a period of immense turmoil and tragedy, especially for the Jewish community. Amidst this chaos, a unique group found themselves in a painfully ironic situation. These were Jewish men who had served in the British military during the war, only to witness Britain's harsh treatment of Holocaust survivors in its aftermath. Their experiences and reactions significantly influenced the subsequent Revolt against the British Mandate in Palestine.

For Jewish British soldiers, witnessing these actions was profoundly distressing. They had just fought alongside the British forces against Nazi Germany, the regime that had orchestrated the Holocaust. To then see the British authorities treating Holocaust survivors with such harshness was seen as a betrayal. Many of these soldiers felt deep anger and disappointment towards the British government. Moreover, these policies brought about a significant conflict of loyalties. On the one hand, these men had served in the British military and deeply respected the rule of law. On the other hand, they were Jewish, and the people suffering under British policies were their relatives who had just endured the unimaginable horrors of the Holocaust.

Impact on the Revolt Against the British Mandate The anger and disillusionment felt by these Jewish British soldiers significantly influenced the Revolt against the British Mandate. Their military training and experience became invaluable assets for the Jewish resistance movements. Many joined underground militias like the Haganah, Irgun, and Lehi, playing critical roles in their operations against the British authorities. Moreover, their firsthand experiences of British policies helped rally support for the resistance within Palestine and internationally. Their stories highlighted the brutality of the British immigration restrictions and internment practices, painting a vivid picture of the suffering endured by Holocaust survivors. This increased public sympathy for the Zionist cause and pressured the British government to alter its policies.

The anguish of Jewish British soldiers caught between their loyalty to the British military and their solidarity with fellow Jews had far-reaching effects on the Revolt against the British Mandate. Their military expertise and emotionally charged experiences fueled the resistance, making them an indispensable part of the struggle for a Jewish state in Palestine.

Chapter#9 The Zionist revolt in Palestine.

Manchan[110] Begin[111], the Leader of Irgun, began a plot for a revolt in Palestine with an insurrection using all of the militia forces in the Zionist culture to fight the British Mandate and the British soldiers and police in Palestine.

, The political landscape in Palestine was marked by intense struggles for power and control. Central to these struggles were two prominent Zionist leaders: David[112] Ben[113]-[114]Gurion[115], the head of the Jewish Agency, and Menachem Begin, the Leader of the Irgun. The conflict between these two leaders over the decision to launch a revolt against the British military Arabs and the Mandate in Palestine. David Ben-Gurion, often regarded as the architect of the State of Israel, believed in a pragmatic approach toward achieving Jewish statehood.

As the head of the Jewish Agency, Ben-Gurion advocated for diplomacy and negotiation with the British authorities. He reasoned that the Jewish community in Palestine was not yet strong enough to confront the British military directly and that a violent uprising could potentially jeopardize international sympathy and support for the Zionist cause. Compared to Ben-Gurion, Menachem Begin, the Leader of the Irgun, advocated for a more militant approach. Begin argued that the British Mandate in Palestine was a colonial regime that oppressed the Jewish people.

---

110. http://www.ibiblio.org/sullivan/bios/MenachemBegin-Bio.html

111. http://www.ibiblio.org/sullivan/bios/MenachemBegin-Bio.html

112. https://www.britannica.com/biography/David-Ben-Gurion

113. https://www.britannica.com/biography/David-Ben-Gurion

114. https://www.britannica.com/biography/David-Ben-Gurion

115. https://www.britannica.com/biography/David-Ben-Gurion

He believed that only through armed resistance could the Jewish community assert its right to self-determination and establish an independent Jewish state.

The Irgun, under Begin's leadership, initiated a series of attacks against British military targets and infrastructure, marking the start of the Revolt. (29) The decision to launch a revolt against the British military and the Mandate in Palestine led to a deep schism between Ben-Gurion and Begin. Ben-Gurion, fearing that the Revolt could lead to a full-scale war that the Jewish community was not prepared for, publicly denounced Begin and the Irgun. He went as far as to cooperate with British authorities in their efforts to suppress the Irgun and Lehi. This move earned him the ire of more militant factions within the Zionist movement. On the other hand, Begin argued that Ben-Gurion's approach was overly cautious and that his willingness to negotiate with the British was a capitulation.

The Irgun continued its resistance campaign, further escalating tensions between the two leaders and their respective factions.

The[116]assassination[117]of[118]Lord[119]Moyne[120],

[121]the[122]British[123]Minister[124]of[125]State[126]in[127]the[128]Middle[129]East[130],

---

116. https://archive.org/details/isbn_9780791083093/page/37

117. https://archive.org/details/isbn_9780791083093/page/37

118. https://archive.org/details/isbn_9780791083093/page/37

119. https://archive.org/details/isbn_9780791083093/page/37

120. https://archive.org/details/isbn_9780791083093/page/37

121. https://archive.org/details/isbn_9780791083093/page/37

122. https://archive.org/details/isbn_9780791083093/page/37

123. https://archive.org/details/isbn_9780791083093/page/37

124. https://archive.org/details/isbn_9780791083093/page/37

125. https://archive.org/details/isbn_9780791083093/page/37

126. https://archive.org/details/isbn_9780791083093/page/37

127. https://archive.org/details/isbn_9780791083093/page/37

128. https://archive.org/details/isbn_9780791083093/page/37

[131]in[132] 1944[133] by Lehi sent shockwaves through the Jewish community in Palestine and beyond. As a key figure in enforcing the British Mandate's "White Paper" policy Lord Moyne became the target of Irgun and Lehi . He enforce the policies which severely restricted Jewish immigration to Palestine during the Second World War Lord Moyne had been widely accused of being responsible for the deaths of thousands of Jews who could have found refuge from the Holocaust in Palestine. His policies were seen as not only anti-Semitic but also pro-Arab, adding fuel to the growing fire of Jewish resistance against British rule. The Jewish Agency, the main representative body of the Jewish community in Palestine, found itself in a challenging position following Lord Moyne's assassination. On the one hand, it was under pressure from more radical elements within the Zionist movement, such as the underground militant groups the Irgun and the Lehi, who saw the assassination as a justified act of resistance against a figure who embodied the oppressive British policies that were jeopardizing Jewish lives. The political moderates also questioned the Jewish Agency's power against the British, who planned to continue the Mandate.

The Jewish Agency was aware of the potential backlash from the British authorities and the international community, which could harm the Zionist cause. In response to this complex situation, the Jewish Agency condemned the assassination. Its leaders, including David Ben-Gurion, knew they needed to distance themselves from such acts of violence to maintain international sympathy and support for their cause.

---

129. https://archive.org/details/isbn_9780791083093/page/37

130. https://archive.org/details/isbn_9780791083093/page/37

131. https://archive.org/details/isbn_9780791083093/page/37

132. https://archive.org/details/isbn_9780791083093/page/37

133. https://archive.org/details/isbn_9780791083093/page/37

They feared that the assassination could be used by the British authorities to crack down on the Jewish community in Palestine and to portray the Zionist movement as a terrorist organization in the international arena. However, while publicly condemning the assassination, the Jewish Agency also used it as an opportunity to draw attention to the dire situation of European Jewry and the role the British policies had played in exacerbating it. They highlighted the desperation and frustration that had driven some Jews to resort to such extreme measures and called for a reassessment of the British policies in Palestine.

The assassination of Lord Moyne and the Jewish Agency's response to it marked a critical juncture in the history of the Zionist movement. They underscored the deep divisions within the Jewish community in Palestine over the methods and strategies to be used in the struggle for a Jewish state.

The Jewish Agency was determined to control the attacks by Irgun and Lehi and the "hunting season "or the "Saison," was created with the Haganah forces to negotiate a plan, The revisionists rejected it. Begin, and Lehi's leadership rejected this plan. The assassination of the British Resident Minister of State,Lord[134]Moyne[135], by Lehi members Eliyahu Hakim and Eliyahu Bet-Zuri on November 6, 1944, triggered a series of events thatbegan "Saison,"

The Saison, or "[136]Hunting[137] Season[138],"[139] was a campaign initiated by the Jewish Agency to root out and neutralize the extremist underground groups, particularly the Lehi and the Irgun. The operation was conducted primarily by members of the Haganah, the

---

134. https://www.timesofisrael.com/yitzhak-shamir-why-we-killed-lord-moyne/

135. https://www.timesofisrael.com/yitzhak-shamir-why-we-killed-lord-moyne/

136. https://etzel.org.il/english/ac07.htm

137. https://etzel.org.il/english/ac07.htm

138. https://etzel.org.il/english/ac07.htm

139. https://etzel.org.il/english/ac07.htm

Jewish paramilitary organization, and its intelligence unit, the Shai, as well as the elite strike force known as the Palmach. (30)

The Jewish Agency's decision to collaborate with the British authorities in this campaign was highly controversial. Haganah members were tasked with gathering intelligence on the activities of Lehi and Irgun members, leading to the arrest and imprisonment of many of their fellow citizens by the British. The men selected for this operation were often faced with the complex moral dilemma of betraying their fellow Jews to the British. This choice sowed deep divisions within the Jewish community.

The campaign successfully curbed Lehi and Irgun's activities, temporarily. Many of their leaders were arrested, and the operations of these groups were significantly disrupted. However, the Saison was eliminate by The Jewish Agency accepted that British Mandate rules was more of a threat to creation of a Jewish state and only a revolt would force them to end the Mandate. the actions of Terrorism .the radical elements, and both Lehi and Irgun would later play crucial roles in the final years leading up to the establishment of the State of Israel.

On August 25, 1945, the British Colonial Office informed **Chaim Weizmann**, the leader of the Zionist movement, that the Jewish immigration quota would not be increased following the end of world war 2.

This decision came when the need for a haven for the Jewish people, many of whom were survivors of the Holocaust, was more pressing than ever. The Jewish community viewed as a betrayal the British stance, and it created a sense of urgency and desperation that sparked radical responses.

Because of the British decision, the Jewish Agency, which had primarily been engaged in diplomatic negotiations, began to consider military action. Pressure mounted within the ranks of the Haganah, the largest Jewish paramilitary organization in Palestine, to strike at the British. This represented a significant shift in the Haganah's stance, which had previously refrained from direct confrontations with the British authorities.

Chapter #10

The Jewish Resistance Movement.

The Haganah, Irgun, and Lehi, In light of the British Colonial Office's Plan to continue the limits on Jewish immigration to Palestine, found that the Jewish Agency had shifted their policy toward diplomacy with the British. The Jewish Agency reached out to Irgun and Lehi, the prominent Jewish paramilitary organizations known for their radical ideologies and aggressive tactics. The aim was to form a united front against the British, and negotiations between these groups began in August 1945. After several discussions, at the end of October 1945, the Haganah, Irgun, and Lehi joined to form the Jewish Resistance Movement.(31)The formation of the Jewish Resistance Movement marked a significant escalation in the Jewish-Arab conflict. With this alliance, the Jewish resistance against the British became more organized, strategic, and forceful. The Jewish Resistance Movement carried out a series of attacks against British targets, significantly straining the relations between the British authorities and the Jewish community.

One of the key events that marked this period was the **'Night of the Trains'** attack orchestrated by Haganah,(32)

During the 'Night of the Trains' attacks train stations , The "Night of the Trains" was a significant turning point in the Jewish Resistance Movement's struggle against British rule in Mandate Palestine. Taking place on November 1, 1945, this coordinated sabotage operation targeted the British-controlled railway infrastructure, a vital part of Palestine's transport system. Around 1,000 fighters from various resistance groups, including Palmach, Irgun, and Lehi, were involved in the operation, which inflicted severe damage on 153 points along the railway system. These acts disrupted key transportation routes at junctions and bridges, severely undermining British logistical capabilities. Additionally, Palmach forces blew up three British guard boats in the ports of Jaffa and Haifa, further destabilizing British authority.

The operation was notable not just for its scale, but also for its symbolic significance. It was one of the earliest major actions carried out by the Jewish Resistance Movement, signaling the movement's resolve to challenge British rule and paving the way for future operations aimed at weakening the British mandate. The attack on the Lydda railway station, a critical junction connecting key lines, underscored the strategic precision of the resistance. The success of the Night of the Trains marked a decisive moment in the broader Palestinian revolts and resistance efforts. It both galvanized Jewish fighters and sent a strong message to the British, highlighting the growing opposition to British policies and the intensifying struggle for control over Palestine.

The British authorities implemented several immediate measures to mitigate the damage and restore order. These included ramping up security measures across Palestine, particularly around key infrastructure sites. British authorities also initiated a widespread manhunt to apprehend those responsible for the attacks. This led to numerous arrests and detentions, often conducted on a large scale and targeting Jewish communities known for their support or sympathy towards the revolt.

The[140]Morrison[141]-[142]Grady[143]Plan[144]Following the attacks, the British government began reassessing its policy in PalestineThe 'Night of the

---

140. https://en.wikipedia.org/wiki/Morrison%E2%80%93Grady_Plan

141. https://en.wikipedia.org/wiki/Morrison%E2%80%93Grady_Plan

142. https://en.wikipedia.org/wiki/Morrison%E2%80%93Grady_Plan

143. https://en.wikipedia.org/wiki/Morrison%E2%80%93Grady_Plan

Trains' attacks exposed the vulnerability of British control and the growing threat posed by Jewish paramilitary organizations.(33) The British government proposed the Morrison-Grady Plan in 1946 to address these issues. This Plan, named after British Foreign Secretary Herbert Morrison and American diplomat Henry Grady, proposed the establishment of a federal state within Palestine, with separate provinces for Jews and Arabs.

The Plan aimed to limit conflicts between the two communities while maintaining overall British control. However, it was met with significant resistance from Jewish and Arab leaders and eventually shelved.

The Yeshiva's Reaction to the British Government's New Policy on Palestine British Foreign Secretary Ernest Bevin presented the British government's new policy on Palestine in a speech to the House of Commons. Different sections of the Jewish community have had varied reactions to this policy, which was viewed as a critical turning point in the ongoing conflict. The Blevins Plan, proposed in 1947 by British Foreign Secretary Ernest Bevin, aimed to address the escalating tensions in Palestine between Jews and Arabs under British rule. The plan outlined a five-year trusteeship regime, during which Britain would oversee the territory, allowing 4,000 Jewish immigrants per month for two years. After this period, there would be a possibility of Palestine gaining independence at the end of the five-year term. However, the plan was rejected by both Jewish and Arab communities for different reasons.

The response of the Yeshiva, a Jewish educational institution, to this landmark policy. When Ernest Bevin unveiled the new British policy regarding Palestine, it came as a shock to many within the Jewish community, not the least to the Yeshiva.

---

144. https://en.wikipedia.org/wiki/Morrison%E2%80%93Grady_Plan

It was seen as a departure from the Balfour Declaration of 1917 and perceived as a potential threat to the Jewish community's dreams of a homeland in Palestine.(34)

Bevin's policy's unveiling ignited a fierce debate within the Yeshiva. The scholars and students grappled with the potential effects of this policy on their community and their long-cherished hope for a Jewish state.

The Bevin statement needed to meet these expectations. Instead, it proposed the creation of a bi national state in Palestine and limited Jewish immigration to the region. The Jewish community saw the Bevin statement as a betrayal by the British government.

They argued that it ignored the historical and spiritual connection of the Jewish people to the land of Palestine, as well as their need for a safe haven in the wake of the Holocaust. Jewish groups in Palestine, including the Haganah and the Irgun, responded with attacks against British targets in what came to be known as the Jewish Insurgency in Palestine.

On the other hand, the Bevin statement was met with a more positive response from the Arab leaders in Palestine. They saw it as a recognition of their opposition to unrestricted Jewish immigration and the establishment of a Jewish state in Palestine. The Bevin statement's proposal for a binational state and limited Jewish immigration aligned with their goals. However, the Arab leaders also had reservations about the Bevin statement. They were skeptical about the British government's intentions and commitment to implementing the proposals.

They saw the continued British Mandate as an obstacle to Arab independence and self-determination.

The Bevin statement elicited strong reactions from both the Jewish and Arab communities in Palestine. It deepened the divide between the two communities and added to the complexity of the Palestine question. The reactions to the Bevin statement underscore the

deep-seated and conflicting aspirations of the Jewish and Arab
communities in Palestine, a conflict that continues to shape the
region's history. The Bevin Statement incited riots across Palestine.
Jewish groups, enraged by what they perceived as a betrayal by the
British, took to the streets in protest.

The riots were characterized by widespread civil unrest, with violent
clashes between protesters and British forces. The Arab community
also engaged in protests, fearful of losing their majority status and the
potential establishment of a Jewish state in Palestine.

In response to the Bevin Statement and the perceived betrayal by the
British, various resistance movements began planning attacks against
the British.

The Jewish resistance movement, notably groups like the Haganah,
Irgun, and Lehi, started organizing a united front against the British
Mandate. The Haganah, the largest of these groups, initially focused
on defense tactics but soon adopted a more aggressive approach. They
planned attacks on British installations, aiming to disrupt British
governance and control over Palestine.

The Irgun and Lehi, more radical in their approach, also planned and
executed several attacks against British forces. The unrest forced the
British to reassess their policies, leading to the referral of the Palestine
issue to the United Nations in 1947.

The subsequent search operations conducted by British troops and
police against Jewish settlements, including Givat Haim, Hogla,
Shefayim, and Rishpon, further escalated the situation. Tensions
between the British authorities, Jewish settlers, and the Arab
population were at an all-time high. The catalyst for the November
riots was a series of attacks on government buildings, which quickly
spilled over into widespread unrest in major cities. Tel Aviv, a
significant cultural and economic hub, was particularly affected. The
authorities responded by imposing a strict curfew to regain control
and prevent further violence.

In the aftermath of the riots and the imposition of curfews, British troops and police conducted extensive search operations on November 25 and 26 against Jewish settlements.(35)These operations were met with violent resistance from Jewish civilians, further escalating tensions and leading to several clashes.

The November riots and the subsequent search operations marked a significant escalation in the Jewish-Arab conflict in the Middle East. The violent resistance from Jewish civilians during the search operations underscored the deep-seated resentment and defiance towards British authority and their handling of the situation. These events further strained relations between the British, Jewish, and Arab communities,

They underscored the deep-seated tensions and conflicts in the region, particularly between the British authorities, Jewish settlers, and the Arab population.

The emergence of a fresh wave of violence as terrorist actions aimed at disrupting the infrastructure and turning Palestine into a combat zone had a profound impact on the eventual untimely end of the British Mandate before 1948.These were not random acts of violence, but meticulously planned attacks aimed at destabilizing the region. Key targets included weapons depots, airfields, railway stations, and communication hubs. The intent was dual-pronged: to equip themselves with weapons for their armed struggle and to cripple the region's infrastructure.

These terrorist actions posed a significant challenge to the British administration. The increasing violence made it incredibly difficult to maintain law and order. The attacks disrupted transportation and communication, impacting trade, administration, and military operations.

Faced with the escalating violence, the mounting costs of maintaining control over Palestine, and the growing international and domestic pressure, the British government decided to refer the issue of Palestine to the United Nations in 1947.(36)This led to the proposal of the partition plan, which was approved by the U.N. General Assembly in November 1947.(37)

Chapter #11

The End of the British Mandate

The U.N. determined the British could not maintain the Mandate effectively a midst the violence and chaos; Britain announced the termination of its Mandate by August 1948, a decision that came earlier than initially envisioned. Thus, the increase in terrorist activities significantly contributed to the early end of the British Mandate in Palestine.

The High Commissioner Alan[145]Cunningham[146] decided to move against the Jewish Agency and Haganah. As a result, the British planned a massive military and police operation called Operation[147]Agatha[148], under which Jewish institutions and settlements would be raided, and mass arrests carried out against Jewish leaders and Haganah members.

High Commissioner Alan Cunningham's decision to launch "Operation Agatha," more infamously known as the "Black Sabbath", was a pivotal move in the turbulent era of British Palestine.(38)Cunningham was at the helm of the British administration in Palestine during heightened tension and violence. With Jewish paramilitary groups escalating their attacks against the British, Cunningham found himself in a precarious position. The British government, while committed to maintaining law and order in Palestine, was under significant pressure both internationally and domestically to quell the violence without resorting to extreme measures. Cunningham, tasked with navigating this complex scenario,

---

145. https://en.wikipedia.org/wiki/Alan_Cunningham

146. https://en.wikipedia.org/wiki/Alan_Cunningham

147. https://en.wikipedia.org/wiki/Operation_Agatha

148. https://en.wikipedia.org/wiki/Operation_Agatha

hoped that Operation Agatha would serve as a decisive move to regain control of the region.

The operation, which involved a massive crackdown on Jewish settlements, was aimed at rooting out members of the resistance and seizing weapons and intelligence documents. The Athena team, a group of skilled intelligence officers, was at the forefront of this operation. Their task was to search for documents that would expose the Jewish Agency's involvement in the resistance, thereby providing the British authorities with the evidence to justify their actions and potentially weaken the resistance movement. Cunningham hoped that by implicating the Jewish Agency, a critical political entity representing the Jewish community in Palestine, the British could drive a wedge between the political leadership and the more radical elements within the community. He believed this would diminish support for the resistance, undermining their capacity to carry out attacks against the British.

Furthermore, Cunningham expected the operation to send a clear message to the Jewish community and the international audience. By demonstrating the British administration's resolve and capacity to respond decisively to the escalating violence, he hoped to deter further attacks and garner support for the British Mandate in Palestine. However, Operation Agatha did not unfold as Cunningham had expected. The Jewish community responded with outrage, and the operation only served to escalate tensions between the British authorities and the Jewish community in Palestine. Internationally, the brutal crackdown drew widespread criticism, further straining Britain's position.

While High Commissioner Alan Cunningham launched **Operation Agatha** with the expectation of regaining control over the escalating violence in Palestine and exposing the Jewish Agency's involvement in the resistance, the operation had unintended consequences. Instead of dampening the resistance, it served to intensify the conflict.

The Yishiva and Jewish Agency were raided as a part of the "Black Sabbath." the British used 10,000 troops on the Sabbath raid to search for arms and made arrests in Jerusalem[149], Tel[150]Aviv[151], Haifa[152], and several dozen settlements; the Jewish[153]Agency[154] was raided.(39)The total number of British security forces involved is reported to be as high as 25,000. About 2,700 individuals were arrested. The goal was to end the state of anarchy in Palestine and prove the Haganah and their particular operations were directed by the Jewish Agency.

The operation wanted to have documentary proof of Jewish Agency approval of sabotage operations by the Palmach[155] and of an alliance between the Haganah[156] and the more violent Lehi[157] (Stern Gang) and Irgun.

There were mass arrests of Palmach and Jewish Agency members during the operation; the leader of the Jewish Agency, David Ben-Gurion, escaped to Paris. The operation ended on July 1. It was successful in causing the Haganah and Palmach to back off on military operations without the support of the Jewish Agency; however, it tightly joined the Irgun and Stern gang. The taking of information from the Jewish Agency exposed their members and plans and led to the arrest by the British police and the military. There were plans of executions for treason of Jews who were collaborators with the British and informants.

---

149. https://en.wikipedia.org/wiki/Jerusalem

150. https://en.wikipedia.org/wiki/Tel_Aviv

151. https://en.wikipedia.org/wiki/Tel_Aviv

152. https://en.wikipedia.org/wiki/Haifa

153. https://en.wikipedia.org/wiki/Jewish_Agency

154. https://en.wikipedia.org/wiki/Jewish_Agency

155. https://en.wikipedia.org/wiki/Palmach

156. https://en.wikipedia.org/wiki/Haganah

157. https://en.wikipedia.org/wiki/Lehi_(group)

Irgrun began a wave of murders and planned kidnappings after Operation Agatha that forced High Commissioner Alan[158]Cunningham[159] to commute the Irgun members' with a death sentences to life imprisonment.

But Menachem[160]Begin[161] believed that Irgun and the Stern gang needed to prevent the British from using the information taken during Agatha. Thus, a plan was created to destroy the British command and attack the center of its power, the King David Hotel(40)

On July 22, 1946, Jerusalem experienced one of the most significant events in the history of combat in Palestine. The King David Hotel, serving as the British administrative headquarters, was attacked by the Irgun, who organized the attack.(41)This attack was not just an act of resistance against the British Mandate in Palestine but also a strategic move in the context of the ongoing struggle for Jewish statehood. The King David Hotel housed not only the British administrative offices but also significant amounts of intelligence information that could be used against the Jewish Agency, the main body leading the Zionist movement. The Irgun hoped that by destroying the hotel, they could prevent the British from leveraging this information against the Jewish Agency and the broader Zionist cause. The planning and execution of the attack were characterized by a combination of meticulous planning and audacious execution. The Irgun operatives infiltrated the hotel disguised as Arab workers, planting explosives in the basement. The subsequent explosion resulted in significant loss of life and property, marking a turning point in the Jewish resistance against British rule. The attack on the King David Hotel was a clear signal of the Irgun's determination and capacity to challenge British authority. It demonstrated the Jewish resistance's capability to strike at the heart

---

158. https://en.wikipedia.org/wiki/Alan_Cunningham

159. https://en.wikipedia.org/wiki/Alan_Cunningham

160. https://en.wikipedia.org/wiki/Menachem_Begin

161. https://en.wikipedia.org/wiki/Menachem_Begin

of the British administration. The hope was that this show of force would deter the British from their attempts to suppress Jewish immigration and aspirations for statehood. However, alongside these strategic considerations, the attack on the King David Hotel was also a source of controversy and division within the Jewish community. The use of such violent tactics was seen by many as a departure from the principles of the Zionist movement. Critics argued that the attack undermined the moral high ground that the Jewish cause had held in its struggle for statehood.

Despite these criticisms, Irgun believed that the attack was a necessary measure in the face of British policy in Palestine. They argued that the British were suppressing Jewish immigration and undermining the possibility of a Jewish state, and as such, drastic measures were necessary to protect the Zionist cause. The attack on the King David Hotel by the Irgun was a significant event in the history of the Jewish struggle for statehood.

It was a demonstration of the willingness and capacity of the Jewish resistance to challenge British authority. Ninety-one people were killed, most of them being staff of the hotel or Secretariat: 21 were first-rank government officials; 49 were second-rank clerks, typists and messengers, junior members of the Secretariat, employees of the hotel and canteen workers; 13 were soldiers; 3 policemen; and 5 were bystanders. By nationality, there were 41 Arabs, 28 British citizens, 17 Jews, 2 Armenians, 1 Russian, 1 Greek and 1 Egyptian. Forty-nine people were injured.

The attack resulted in worldwide condemnation, but Menachem Begin and moderate Zionists believed that this was now a part of the conflict in the future.(42) The Irgun accepted that it had bombed the hotel but that the British had ignored their warnings.

But The claim was dismissed by Chief Secretary Sir John Shaw, who was in his office at the time of the bombing.(43)

To gain control over the situation, the British military began what was known as **Operation Shark**.

Operation Shark, a military operation launched in retaliation for the attack on the King David Hotel, marked a significant turning point in British Mandatory Palestine. The attack on the hotel, orchestrated by the Jewish paramilitary organization Irgun, was a direct act of defiance against British rule in Palestine. It sent shockwaves through the British administration, both in Palestine and back in Britain. The British authorities were determined to respond decisively.(44)

Operation Shark was launched with the intent to dismantle the militant Zionist underground involved in the bombing at the King David Hotel.The operation was characterized by raids and arrests aimed at rooting out resistance members and curtailing their operations. It demonstrated the British authority was determined to resolve and maintain control and restore order in Palestine. However, the operation did not go as planned. The Jewish community in Palestine rallied around the resistance, viewing Operation Shark as an act of oppression. The operation sparked widespread protests and acts of defiance, further escalating the tensions between the Jewish community Arabs the public and the British authorities. Back in Britain, the news of Operation Shark and the escalating violence in Palestine was met with growing concern. Still recovering from the aftermath of World War II, the British public began to question the wisdom of maintaining the Mandate a midst such hostility.

The operation, intended to quell the resistance and restore order, had instead fueled the flames of conflict. This turning point led to a shift in British policy towards Palestine. Faced with growing unrest and increasing international pressure, the British government began reconsidering its position on the Mandate. This eventually led to the decision to end the British Mandate in Palestine, a move that set the stage for the creation of the state of Israel. Operation Shark, launched in retaliation for the attack on the King David Hotel, was ended and the supression by the British was ended . It marked a turning point in British Mandatory Palestine, leading to a shift in British policy and playing a significant role in the eventual end of the Mandate.

The groups of the resistance continued the attacks on the British military with shootings of individual soldiers and police officers while walking in the cities of Palestine. On August 31 the Irgun attacked the British embassy in Rome, and on November 9–13 – Jewish underground members launched a series of land mine and suitcase bomb attacks against railroad stations, trains, and streetcars, killing 11 British soldiers and policemen and 8 Arab constables.

The Irgun and Stern gang killed British soldiers at their homes and workplaces at any location where British police or military officers met.

• The terrorists focused the attacks on British military bases, seaports with naval vessels, and vessels used to transport illegal immigrants to Cyprus for detention. March 12 – Irgun attacked the Schneller[162]Camp[163], which was being used as a barracks and office of the Royal Army Pay Corps. One British soldier was killed, and eight were wounded. A British camp near Karkur[164] was also raided, shots were fired at the Sarona[165] camp, and a mine exploded near Rishon LeZion. The Jewish immigrant ship Theodore *Herzl* was captured by the British Navy and routed to Cyprus.

April 19 – Four Irgun fighters (Dov[166]Gruner[167], Yehiel[168]Dresner[169], Mordechai[170]Alkahi[171], and Eliezer[172]Kashani[173]) were hanged by

---

162. https://en.wikipedia.org/wiki/Schneller_Orphanage

163. https://en.wikipedia.org/wiki/Schneller_Orphanage

164. https://en.wikipedia.org/wiki/Pardes_Hanna-Karkur

165. https://en.wikipedia.org/wiki/Sarona_(colony)

166. https://en.wikipedia.org/wiki/Dov_Gruner

British authorities. Irgun retaliated with three attacks; a British soldier was killed during a raid on a field dressing station near Netanya[174], General Evelyn Barker was the General[175]Officer[176]Commanding[177] (GOC) of the British[178]Forces[179]in[180]Palestine[181]and[182]Trans[183]-[184]Jordan[185] from 1946 to 1947. He signed the death warrants, knowing that Irgun and Stern gang would retaliate. None of the men who were hanged asked for their sentence to be commuted or provided a defense, except they claimed that the British were on their land and they needed to be removed even if they were killed. Barker believed that The terrorists were a part of a team of murderers and not soldiers defending freedom fighters.. Barker took the attack by terrorists as a personal mark against

167. https://en.wikipedia.org/wiki/Dov_Gruner

168. https://en.wikipedia.org/wiki/Yehiel_Dresner

169. https://en.wikipedia.org/wiki/Yehiel_Dresner

170. https://en.wikipedia.org/wiki/Mordechai_Alkahi

171. https://en.wikipedia.org/wiki/Mordechai_Alkahi

172. https://en.wikipedia.org/wiki/Eliezer_Kashani

173. https://en.wikipedia.org/wiki/Eliezer_Kashani

174. https://en.wikipedia.org/wiki/Netanya

175. https://en.wikipedia.org/wiki/General_Officer_Commanding

176. https://en.wikipedia.org/wiki/General_Officer_Commanding

177. https://en.wikipedia.org/wiki/General_Officer_Commanding

178. https://en.wikipedia.org/wiki/Palestine_Command

179. https://en.wikipedia.org/wiki/Palestine_Command

180. https://en.wikipedia.org/wiki/Palestine_Command

181. https://en.wikipedia.org/wiki/Palestine_Command

182. https://en.wikipedia.org/wiki/Palestine_Command

183. https://en.wikipedia.org/wiki/Palestine_Command

184. https://en.wikipedia.org/wiki/Palestine_Command

185. https://en.wikipedia.org/wiki/Palestine_Command

his leadership and British authority, and there was no need for clemency for murder.

General Evelyn Barker felt that the failure to use capital punishment for Zionist guerillas was the reason that the insurgency occurred and that even if there was a threat to murder British officers, the executions must be done. Barker was accused of being anti-Semitic for the harsh rules he imposed on the Jews as a result of the insurgency and the bombing attack on the King David Hotel. The British searched every home in Tel Aviv.

the most important figure of the Zionist underground, Menachem[186]Begin[187], went into hiding and he was the most wanted Terrorist in Palestine.

Begin claimed that the members of Irgun and Stern gang were soldiers and POWs, and the British government had no right to execute them or court martial them even if British soldiers were killed.

Menachem Begin's Retaliation Strategy

• On April 19, Four Irgun fighters (Dov[188]Gruner[189], Yehiel[190]Dresner[191], Mordechai[192]Alkahi[193], and Eliezer[194]Kashani[195]) were hanged by British authorities. These executions marked a turning point in retaliations in the conflict.

---

186. https://en.wikipedia.org/wiki/Menachem_Begin

187. https://en.wikipedia.org/wiki/Menachem_Begin

188. https://en.wikipedia.org/wiki/Dov_Gruner

189. https://en.wikipedia.org/wiki/Dov_Gruner

190. https://en.wikipedia.org/wiki/Yehiel_Dresner

191. https://en.wikipedia.org/wiki/Yehiel_Dresner

192. https://en.wikipedia.org/wiki/Mordechai_Alkahi

193. https://en.wikipedia.org/wiki/Mordechai_Alkahi

194. https://en.wikipedia.org/wiki/Eliezer_Kashani

195. https://en.wikipedia.org/wiki/Eliezer_Kashani

This execution began as several attacks at specific targets selected to cause the British military and police a state of fear. In 1947, on January 5 – Eleven British soldiers were injured in a grenade attack on a train in Banha[196] carrying British troops to Palestine from Egypt[197]. This was followed by March 1 when Irgun bombed the Officer's Club on King[198]George[199]Street[200] in Jerusalem, killing 17 British officers and wounding 27, resulting in martial[201]law[202] that lasted 16 days.

The retaliation by the Irgun, a Zionist paramilitary organization, following the execution of two of its members, Sergeants Clifford Martin and Mervyn Paice, by the British authorities. The incident, known as the Sergeants affair, had far-reaching implications, causing a anger in Britain and among Zionist defenders. In the summer of 1947, the Irgun, led by Menachem Begin, captured two British sergeants in retaliation for the British authorities' sentencing and execution of three Irgun members. The two sergeants, Clifford Martin and Mervyn Paice, were subsequently hanged by the Irgun after the British carried out the execution of the Irgun members. (45)
The bodies of the two sergeants were booby-trapped and left hanging in a eucalyptus grove near Netanya. This violent act of retaliation by the Irgun sparked widespread outrage and led to significant repercussions, both in Britain and within the Zionist movement.

---

196. https://en.wikipedia.org/wiki/Banha

197. https://en.wikipedia.org/wiki/Egypt

198. https://en.wikipedia.org/wiki/King_George_Street_(Jerusalem)

199. https://en.wikipedia.org/wiki/King_George_Street_(Jerusalem)

200. https://en.wikipedia.org/wiki/King_George_Street_(Jerusalem)

201. https://en.wikipedia.org/wiki/Martial_law

202. https://en.wikipedia.org/wiki/Martial_law

The reaction in Britain to the Sergeants affair was one of shock and anger. The brutal nature of the retaliation, particularly the booby-trapping of the sergeants' bodies, led to widespread public outrage. The British press condemned the act, with newspapers like The London Times calling it a "barbarous act of terrorism." There were also several anti-Jewish riots in the U.K. in response to the hangings, with Jewish properties being attacked and vandalized. Politically, the incident put the British government under immense pressure. It led to increased calls for the government to find a solution to the Palestine issue.

The incident is often cited as one of the factors that led to the British government's decision to refer the issue of Palestine to the United Nations, effectively ending their Mandate. Among the defenders of Zionism, the reaction to the Sergeants affair was mixed. While some defended Irgun's actions as a necessary response to British repression, others denounced the act as a hindrance to their cause. The mainstream Zionist leadership, including David Ben-Gurion, the head of the Jewish Agency, condemned Irgun's actions. (46) They were concerned that such acts of violence would tarnish the image of the Zionist movement and alienate international support, particularly from Britain and the United States. However, within the more militant segments of the Zionist movement, there was support for the Irgun's retaliation.

They viewed the act as a legitimate act of resistance against British rule and a response to what they saw as the unjust execution of their members. The retaliation by the Irgun in the aftermath of the hanging of the two sergeants in July 1947 sparked widespread reactions both in Britain and among the defenders of Zionism. The incident led to a rise in anti-Jewish sentiment in Britain and increased pressure on the British government to find a solution to the Palestine issue. Within the Zionist movement, the incident highlighted the rift between the mainstream leadership and the more militant factions, with differing views on the use of violence in the pursuit of their objectives.

The violence that later emerged was angry British soldiers in confrontation with Jews in Tel Aviv throwing stones while many were beaten in the streets. On August 5, the British arrested 35 Jewish political leaders in Palestine, all of whom were members of the Revisionist[203] Party or the right-wing branch of the General Zionists' Party. All Palestinian Jews were forbidden to leave the country until further notice. A long-standing plan to outlaw the Revisionist youth movement Betar[204] as a fertile recruiting ground for the Irgun and Lehi was implemented.

The British were subject to more significant pressure to end the Mandate and return control over Palestine to the United Nations. The leaders of the Irgun and Stern gangs faced no control over their actions. They had become the leader in the attacks on the British, and the Huganah were still controlled by the Jewish Agency. Menachem[205]Begin[206] claimed in his book *The Revolt* that the "cruel act" was one of the events that tipped the balance in the British withdrawal from Palestine. The British government refused to end the capital punishment for terrorism in Palestine, and Begin promised he would find police officers and military to hang as retaliation. (47) The British made a bold decision to bring in a covert expert to strike a blow that would destroy the terrorists. The resistance led by the Irgrun and Stern gang created abduction squads to find British soldiers and police who could be kidnapped and then hanged if the British executed a terrorist.

Chapter # 12

Chapter # 12 The British Counter Insurgency Plot 1947.

---

203. https://en.wikipedia.org/wiki/Revisionist_Zionism

204. https://en.wikipedia.org/wiki/Betar

205. https://en.wikipedia.org/wiki/Menachem_Begin

206. https://en.wikipedia.org/wiki/Menachem_Begin

The Military leaders in England and Palestine faced severe criticism regarding the handling of the insurgency and resistance terrorist attacks in 1947.

The bombing of the King David Hotel, the murder of the two sergeants, and the inability to control Irgun or the Stern gang's leaders by the Jewish administrators. The Jews in the larger cities endured curfews and economic hardship, rejected the British authority's martial laws, The Irgun and Stern gangs were able to recruit from former Haganah and youth groups like Bahar for those willing to fight the British and face execution for terrorist attacks.

The attacks on protected military installations, police stations, prisons, and government offices were organized on a strategic order and supported by the Jewish leadership.

The "Anti-Semitic Reactions in Britain Following the Murder of the Two Sergeants, grew and there were protest and threats of violence .There was also a increased voice for a end to the Mandate by British people.

Jewish businesses and properties were targeted in acts of vandalism and violence. Synagogues and Jewish-owned shops faced attacks and desecration, reflecting the anger and frustration of parts of the British populace.

Jews in Britain experienced increased instances of verbal abuse and harassment. Anti-Semitic rhetoric became more pronounced in public discourse, fueled by the sensationalist media portrayal of the incident.The incident also had political repercussions. British politicians and public figures condemned the actions of the Irgun, but some also used the opportunity to criticize the broader Zionist movement. This criticism sometimes blurred the lines between anti-Zionism and anti-Semitism, exacerbating tensions within British society.(48)

The covert attack plan.

Field Marshal Bernard Montgomery requested that the restrictions on force employed in security operations be lifted despite opposition from the Colonial Office and the fact that the Cabinet had signaled an intention to withdraw from Palestine by May 14, 1948. The leadership believed there was a need to stop the insurgency and the leaders before the end of the Mandate.

Former Royal Marine Nicol Gray, the Inspector General of the Palestine Police, sought to find those who could infiltrate the resistance and expose their actions and leaders.

Major Roy Farran to lead a team in a covert effort to find and kill the members of Lehi and Irgun . He was selected based on his wartime exploits of special forces units behind the lines, Brigadier General Bernard Fergusson was in charge of this covert group(49)

General Fergusson a second SAS commando commanders: Alastair MacGregor (then with MI[207]6[208]) to lead a second team with Roy Farran.

The two men established a covert plan to have MacGregor operate in north Palestine and Farran in the south. Fergusson took the Jerusalem squad pending the arrival of a third squad commander; these areas conformed to military zones, not the six Palestine[209]Police[210] districts. Subsequently, Fergusson said the concept was to provoke contact with the resistance (Irgun and Stern gang). Utilizing jeeps, a citrus-fruit delivery truck, and a dry-cleaner's lorry, Farran's team "moved among Jewish civilians in Jewish clothing" and made several arrests in the month they were active. Still, they could not infiltrate the inner circle of the resistance and the leaders and capture or kill them, hoping it would break the morale.

---

207. https://en.wikipedia.org/wiki/MI6

208. https://en.wikipedia.org/wiki/MI6

209. https://en.wikipedia.org/wiki/Palestine_Police

210. https://en.wikipedia.org/wiki/Palestine_Police

The unit was in conflict with the Criminal Investigation Department. The commando unit felt that the British Police in Palestine had security leaks. They refused to share information with the British CID and acted alone in capture and evidence gathering.

Farran developed a rogue plan of kidnapping and forcing known members of the resistance, using any methods to get information from them. On May 6, 1947, 17-year-old Alexander[211]Rubowitz[212]disappeared while putting up posters for the Jewish paramilitary group Lehi[213]. A hat that was found at the location where Rubowitz was abducted a hat was found that contained the name of Farran inside. The Jewish community searched for him, as well as the police. Sir Henry[214]Gurney[215], a British colonial administrator, demanded that Roy Farran be arrested and questioned about the case, but he disappeared. Farran claimed he was being framed and fled to Syria.

The Syrians, who were sympathetic to Farran, offered him political asylum, hoping he would train their troops for special operations against the Zionists. But he was told if he returned, he would not be arrested, Farran did return expecting that he would not be arrested. but he was, and a court martial was begun for the death of Rubowitz. There were two trials for Farran, and both found him not guilty. Bernard[216]Fergusson[217] persuaded Farran to return voluntarily. Farran escaped to Jordan, after a second trial finally returning when he heard of reprisals being planned against British officers.

---

211. https://israeled.org/lehi-teenager-disappears/

212. https://israeled.org/lehi-teenager-disappears/

213. https://en.wikipedia.org/wiki/Lehi_(group)

214. https://en.wikipedia.org/wiki/Henry_Gurney

215. https://en.wikipedia.org/wiki/Henry_Gurney

216. https://en.wikipedia.org/wiki/Bernard_Fergusson,_Baron_Ballantrae

217. https://en.wikipedia.org/wiki/Bernard_Fergusson,_Baron_Ballantrae

• He was brought to trial in a British military court in Jerusalem. Colonel Fergusson, to whom Farran was said to have confessed his guilt, refused to testify because he might incriminate himself. Farran was found not guilty in the trial,

Roy Farran was ordered out of Palestine and returned to England but faced no criminal charges by the government. His return was short-lived, and he began to create a new name for himself politically, but the Stern gang members attempted to assassinate him with a letter bomb and killed his younger brother Francis Rex Farran. Those who were responsible were caught and arrested in England in 1948.
The British military and political leaders had concluded that the any covert means to stop the revolt would fail and the Mandate policy needed to end.
The British began to plan by May 14, to reduce their presence in Palestine, and allowed for the expanding Immigration of Jews to occur. (50)
The Irgun and Stern gang increased their attacks on Arabs and British military positions because there was no policy change on the immigration of Jews allowed to enter Palestine, and few governmental controls in the Mandate had been removed. The British Military ended all attempts at covert attempts to capture the leaders of the Jewish resistance forces many were released from prison despite being convicted of terrorism and murder.
Chapter #13
The United Nation takes control of Palestine.
The British government had also recommended the establishment of a special committee to prepare a report for the General Assembly. The General Assembly adopted the recommendation to set up the UNSCOP[218] to investigate the cause of the conflict in Palestine and, if possible, devise a solution.

---

218. https://en.wikipedia.org/wiki/United_Nations_Partition_Plan_for_Palestine

The Partition Plan: The resolution recommended the creation of independent Arab and Jewish States linked economically[2][219] and a Special International Regime for Jerusalem[220] and its surroundings. The Arab state was to have a territory of 11,100 square kilometers or 42%, the Jewish state territory of 14,100 square kilometers or 56%, while the remaining 2%—comprising the cities of Jerusalem, Bethlehem, and the adjoining area—would become an international zone.

The Plan was generally accepted by the Zionist state. David Ben Gurion and the Jewish Agency accepted this Plan. Still, The Arabic League entirely rejected the Plan and began to plan for a war with the Jews in Palestine with support from the Arab states that surrounded Palestine.

But the U.N. needed, because of the expanding violence that was growing in Palestine, stockpiling of weapons by the Israelis, and external support for the Arabs with soldiers and guns, the Plan had little hope of succeeding in Palestine.

The Arab leadership in Palestine was verbally claiming that they would defeat the Jews and drive them out, and there was no need for the Partition plan.

The U.N. found a mediator to work a plan to support both sides' wants.

They argued that it violated the principles of national[221] self[222]-[223] determination[224] in the U[225].[226]N[227]. [228]charter[229],

---

219. https://en.wikipedia.org/wiki/United_Nations_Partition_Plan_for_Palestine#cite_note-2

220. https://en.wikipedia.org/wiki/Jerusalem

221. https://en.wikipedia.org/wiki/Self-determination

222. https://en.wikipedia.org/wiki/Self-determination

223. https://en.wikipedia.org/wiki/Self-determination

224. https://en.wikipedia.org/wiki/Self-determination

225. https://en.wikipedia.org/wiki/UN_charter

226. https://en.wikipedia.org/wiki/UN_charter

which grants people the right to decide their destiny. Palestinian Arabs opposed the very idea of partition but reiterated that this partition plan was unfair: the majority of the land (56%) would go to a Jewish state when Jews at that stage legally owned only 6–7% of it and remained a minority of the population (33% in 1946).

May 14, 1948: The end of the British Mandate and the creation of the State of Israel.

The British, on May 14, 1948, left Palestine with only limited military or police support. During this period, the Jewish and Arab communities of the British Mandate clashed, while the British organized their withdrawal and intervened only occasionally. In the first two months of the Civil War, around 1,000 people were killed and 2,000 injured.(51)

The results were that the entire region was thrown into an area of civil war for complete control of the region.

The Jewish Agency planned to support the State of Israel after the end of British rule on May 14.

The period prior to the civil war in the British Mandate of Palestine was a time of significant upheaval and conflict, characterized by clashes between the Jewish and Arab communities. As the British prepared for their withdrawal, their interventions became increasingly infrequent, leaving the two communities to their own devices.

The Jewish community's reaction to the Civil War was multifaceted. On one hand, there was a sense of urgency and determination to establish a Jewish state in the face of escalating violence. This determination manifested in several ways, including mobilizing armed forces and strengthening communal ties. Jewish defense organizations like Haganah, Irgun, and Lehi played significant roles during this

---

227. https://en.wikipedia.org/wiki/UN_charter

228. https://en.wikipedia.org/wiki/UN_charter

229. https://en.wikipedia.org/wiki/UN_charter

period. Despite their ideological differences, they all shared a common goal of Jewish statehood and self-determination.

On the other hand, the civil war also brought about a sense of fear and uncertainty within the Jewish community. The escalating violence and the impending withdrawal of British forces raised concerns about the community's ability to defend itself against the increased Arab aggression. The sporadic and often brutal nature of the conflict resulted in widespread anxiety and concern for the future. However, despite the fear and uncertainty, the civil war also fostered a sense of solidarity and resilience within the Jewish community. The shared adversity strengthened communal bonds and galvanized their resolve to establish a Jewish state.

This period saw increased communal efforts, such as fundraising for defense, providing medical services, and organizing civil defense measures.

The beginning of the Palestine Civil War 1948.

This Plan was formulated by the Haganah, the leading Jewish paramilitary organization, as a comprehensive strategy to counter the escalating violence and establish a Jewish state in the wake of the British withdrawal. Plan[230]Dalet[231], also known as Plan D, was initiated in the spring of 1948. It was designed as a strategic response to the increasing attacks from Arab militias and the impending end of the British Mandate. The Plan aimed to secure areas that were allocated to the Jewish state by the United Nations partition plan, as well as areas with significant Jewish populations that fell outside these borders. At the core of Plan Dalet was the intention to secure continuous Jewish control over critical roads, bridges, and strategic points to ensure Jewish communities' safe movement and establish defensible borders for the proposed Jewish state. The Plan also

---

230. https://www.palestine-studies.org/sites/default/files/attachments/jps-articles/Plan%20dalet.pdf

231. https://www.palestine-studies.org/sites/default/files/attachments/jps-articles/Plan%20dalet.pdf

included measures to counter potential military threats from neighboring Arab states.(52)

However, the execution of Plan Dalet was highly controversial, mainly due to the displacement of Palestinian Arab populations. In instances where Arab villages were perceived as hostile or strategically important, Haganah forces were instructed to capture these areas and expel the inhabitants.

This aspect of the Plan has been the subject of much debate, with critics arguing that it amounted to a deliberate policy of ethnic cleansing. Regardless of its controversy, Plan Dalet was instrumental in shaping the course of the Palestine Civil War and the eventual establishment of the State of Israel.

The Jewish community's reaction to the civil war was multifaceted. On the one hand, there was a sense of urgency and determination to establish a Jewish state in the face of escalating violence. This determination manifested in several ways, including mobilizing armed forces and strengthening communal ties. Jewish defense organizations like Haganah, Irgun, and Lehi played significant roles during this period.

On the other hand, the civil war also brought about a sense of fear and uncertainty within the Jewish community. The escalating violence and the impending withdrawal of British forces raised concerns about the community's ability to defend itself against the increased Arab aggression.

The shared adversity strengthened communal bonds and galvanized their resolve to establish a Jewish state. This period saw an increase in communal efforts, such as fundraising for defense, provision of medical services, and the organization of civil defense measures. In instances where Arab villages were perceived as hostile or strategically important, Haganah forces were instructed to capture these areas and expel the inhabitants.

The Deir Yassin massacre, of Arabs which took place on April 9, 1948, during the implementation of Plan Dalet, was a turning point in the conflict between the Jewish and Arab communities in Palestine. This event had profound implications that went far beyond the immediate horror of the massacre itself,

The village was perceived as a strategic point due to its location on high ground overlooking the main highway into Jerusalem. However, the attack quickly devolved into a massacre, with over 100 Palestinian civilians, including women and children, brutally killed. The events of that day were marked by extreme violence and cruelty, leaving a lasting scar on the collective Palestinian psyche. The psychological impact of the Deir Yassin massacre was immense and far-reaching. It generated widespread fear among the Palestinian population, leading to a mass exodus from nearby villages.

This event, more than any other, contributed to the creation of the Palestinian refugee problem, as thousands of Palestinians fled their homes in fear of further violence. The massacre effectively served to clear large parts of Palestine of its Arab inhabitants, making way for the establishment of the Jewish state. The Deir Yassin massacre also had significant implications for the Jewish community. While the attack was carried out by fringe paramilitary groups, it was widely perceived as representative of the broader Jewish community's stance towards the Arab population. This perception alienated international sympathy and support when the Jewish community sought recognition for the newly declared State of Israel.

The capture of Haifa by Jewish forces had a profound and lasting impact on the Arab populace. Haifa, a major urban center with a mixed Arab-Jewish population, was seen as a symbol of coexistence and cultural diversity. Its capture signaled a decisive shift in power dynamics and marked a significant loss for the Palestinian Arabs. The immediate aftermath of the capture was marked by a mass exodus of Arab residents from the city.

It's estimated that tens of thousands of Palestinians fled Haifa, driven by fear of violent reprisals and persecution. This displacement was part of a larger pattern that emerged during this period, often referred to as the **Nakba**[232] or 'catastrophe' by Palestinians. The Nakba saw the displacement of an estimated 700,000 Palestinians from their homes, The loss of Haifa and other urban centers resulted in the systematic loss of Palestinian land. This loss was not just physical but also cultural and symbolic. The displacement of the Arab populace resulted in the erasure of Arab history, culture, and presence in cities like Haifa. This erasure was further cemented by the renaming of streets, landmarks, and towns, a practice aimed at asserting a new Jewish identity on the landscape.

The capture of Haifa and subsequent events sparked fierce resistance among Palestinians. Despite being poorly armed and organized compared to the Jewish forces, Palestinian Arabs and their allies launched a series of counterattacks and resistance efforts. These efforts, however, were largely unsuccessful in reversing the tide of Jewish victories. Despite the imbalance of power, the resistance underscored the depth of Palestinian Arab opposition to what they perceived as a systematic encroachment on their land and rights.

This operation Dani , launched in July 1948, aimed to capture the towns of Lydda and Ramle, which held strategic importance due to their location along the main road to Jerusalem.

In Operation Dani, the Irgun fought alongside the Haganah, the leading Jewish paramilitary organization, despite the ideological differences that often put them at odds with each other. The Irgun was known for its more radical stance and willingness to use violence in pursuit of its objectives, which included not only the establishment of a Jewish state but also the expansion of its borders. The Irgun's involvement in the attack on Lydda was characterized by its aggressive tactics. The organization believed that a swift and decisive victory in

---

232. https://en.wikipedia.org/wiki/Nakba

Lydda would demoralize the Arab forces and pave the way for the capture of Ramle. The Irgun's fighters quickly overtook Lydda, contributing to the city's fall after a brief but intense battle. Irgun's role in Operation Dani also involved controversial actions. Following the capture of Lydda, the city's Palestinian Arab residents were subjected to an expulsion order. Many of these residents were directed towards Bayt Nabala, a nearby village. The expulsion was carried out with a ruthlessness that was consistent with Irgun's hardline approach, but it also sparked outrage and condemnation, both within and outside the Jewish community This mass expulsion, in which an estimated 50,000 to 70,000 Palestinians were forced to leave Lydda and Ramle, is seen as one of the darkest chapters of the 1948 Arab-Israeli War. This event, often referred to as the Nakba, or 'catastrophe,' by Palestinians, is seen as a symbol of the suffering and displacement that they faced due to the establishment of the State of Israel.

The Siege of Jaffa in April-May 1948 marked one of the most critical episodes of the 1948 Arab-Israeli War. Jaffa, a predominantly Palestinian city adjacent to Tel Aviv, was subjected to a prolonged siege by Jewish forces, leading to a significant shift in the demographics of the town. The siege began in late April 1948 the Haganah, launched Operation Bi'ur Chametz. The operation aimed to establish Jewish control over Jaffa, which was a strategic coastal city with a significant Palestinian population. The Haganah bombarded Jaffa with mortars, causing extensive damage to the city's infrastructure and instilling fear among the Palestinian inhabitants. The intense fighting and bombardment led to a mass exodus of the Palestinian population from Jaffa. An estimated 70,000 to 80,000 Palestinians fled the city during the siege, a significant portion of the city's original population of around 100,000. The displacement was primarily driven by fear of further violence, as rumors of massacres in other Palestinian towns, such as Deir Yassin, spread across the region.

The siege ended in early May 1948 with the surrender of the local Arab forces. By this time, Jaffa was depopulated mainly, with only a small number of Palestinians remaining in the city. The majority of the Palestinians who fled Jaffa during the siege ended up in refugee camps in the Gaza Strip and the West Bank or in neighboring Arab countries. In the aftermath of the blockade, Jaffa's demographics changed dramatically. Once a vibrant center of Palestinian culture and commerce, the city was incorporated into the newly established State of Israel. Jewish immigrants moved into the city, filling the homes and neighborhoods left vacant by the displaced Palestinian population.

The impact of the Siege of Jaffa on the Palestinian population was profound and lasting. The displacement of the Palestinians from Jaffa was part of a larger pattern of displacement that occurred during the 1948 Arab-Israeli War.

This event marked a significant loss of Palestinian land and heritage and has been a central issue in the ongoing Israeli-Palestinian conflict. The expulsion of Palestinians from the town of Safed during the 1948 Arab-Israeli War was a significant event that had lasting consequences for the Palestinian community. Safed, a city in the Northern District of Israel, had a substantial Palestinian population before the war. As the conflict intensified, however, the city became a strategic target for Jewish forces. The town's location is perched on a hilltop overlooking the Jordan River Valley, making it a key point of control. The expulsion of Palestinians from Safed began in earnest with Operation Yiftach in May 1948. This operation, led by the Palmach, the elite fighting force of the Haganah, aimed to establish Jewish control over eastern Galilee, including the town of Safed. The operation began with a blockade that isolated the city and cut off its supply routes. This was followed by an intense artillery barrage and an eventual ground assault. As the Jewish forces advanced, the Palestinian residents of Safed were faced with a stark choice: stay and face potential violence or leave their homes in search of safety.

Many chose the latter, and a mass exodus ensued. Families fled with whatever possessions they could carry, leaving homes, businesses, and a way of life they had known for generations. The expulsion was not a systematic, organized process but a chaotic and often terrifying scramble to escape the advancing forces. The majority of the Palestinians from Safed were forced to flee north, towards Lebanon. The journey was dangerous, with families navigating through hostile territory and often coming under fire. Once in Lebanon, many ended up in refugee camps, where they faced harsh living conditions and an uncertain future. However, not all Palestinians from Safed went to Lebanon. Some moved towards the West Bank, under Jordanian control, while others found refuge in Syria. Regardless of where they ended up, the Palestinian refugees from Safed, like other Palestinian refugees from the 1948 war, were not allowed to return to their homes after the conflict ended.(53)

The U.S. recognized Israel's independence in 1948, marking the start of a crucial alliance. In the aftermath of World War II, the U.S. saw Israel as a democratic foothold in the Middle East, an important ally in a region dominated by strategic interests such as oil and political stability. However, the newly formed state of Israel faced immediate threats from its Arab neighbors, making U.S. support essential for its survival and growth. This backing wasn't just about military aid or economic assistance—it was deeply intertwined with the broader geopolitical landscape and humanitarian concerns after the Holocaust. Simultaneously, the cities of Palestine were undergoing a process of decolonization, spearheaded by Jewish paramilitary groups like Haganah, Irgun, and Lehi. These groups, which had been classified as terrorist organizations by the British authorities, were instrumental in expelling the British from Palestine but also in displacing Palestinian Arabs during the creation of the Israeli state. The U.S. faced a delicate balance: while recognizing Israel's right to exist and the necessity of a Jewish homeland, there were growing concerns over the methods

employed by these groups. Their campaigns of violence and intimidation, often directed at both British and Arab populations, led to the forced exodus of many Palestinian inhabitants,
In light of these dynamics, U.S. support for Israel after 1948 was not just a diplomatic decision but also a strategic one, aimed at stabilizing a region in turmoil. By aligning with Israel, the U.S. aimed to counterbalance Soviet influence in the Middle East.

This was particularly important to the U.S., which was keen on limiting Soviet expansion and maintaining access to Middle Eastern oil.
Politically, supporting the establishment of a Jewish state in Palestine was a popular move domestically for the U.S. The horrific revelations of the Holocaust generated sympathy for the Zionist cause among the American public. Moreover, the influential Jewish community in the U.S. was advocating for the creation of Israel. These factors made the support for Israel politically beneficial for American leaders.
Moreover, the U.S. was instrumental in the recognition of Israel as a state. Despite opposition from certain quarters, including within the U.S. State Department, President Harry Truman decided to recognize Israel just minutes after it declared its independence in 1948.
This swift recognition was a significant boost for Israel, which faced immediate military challenges from its Arab neighbors. In addition to political recognition, the U.S. provided Israel with substantial military support. This began with a de facto arms embargo on the region during the 1948 Arab-Israeli War. While this policy was intended to apply to all parties involved in the conflict, in practice, it disadvantaged the Arab states more than Israel, as Israel was able to secure arms shipments from other sources, notably Czechoslovakia.
Later, the U.S. became a major supplier of military aid to Israel, helping it to build one of the most powerful armed forces in the

Middle East. The United States played a critical role in the establishment and early survival of Israel. Driven by a combination of strategic interests, domestic political considerations, and moral imperatives, the U.S. provided essential political and military support to Israel. This support has continued in various forms, making the U.S.-Israel relationship a pivotal element of Middle Eastern politics. Despite reports of ethnic cleansing and displacement of Palestinians, the U.S. did not take substantial action to halt or condemn these actions during the early years of Israel's existence.(54) This lack of action can be partially attributed to the U.S.'s strategic interests in the region and its commitment to the newly established State of Israel. Internationally, the reaction was mixed. While some countries and international bodies expressed concern and condemned the displacement of Palestinians, others were silent or tacitly supportive of Israel. In the face of these reports, the United Nations (U.N.) created the United Nations Relief and Works Agency for Palestine Refugees in the Near East (**UNRWA**[233])[234]

In 1949, to address the growing Palestinian refugee crisis. The UNRWA was tasked with providing aid and support to displaced Palestinians, an explicit acknowledgment of the humanitarian crisis unfolding due to the displacement. However, the creation of the UNRWA did not address the root cause of the displacement, and the international community largely failed to take effective action to stop or reverse the expulsion of Palestinians from their homes. Many Arab nations, on the other hand, were vocally critical of the displacement and alleged ethnic cleansing. They offered support to Palestinian refugees and, in some cases, launched military actions against Israel, which led to further conflicts in the region. However, these actions did not result in any significant change in the situation on the ground. Overall, the global reaction to the ethnic cleansing of Palestine

---

233. https://en.wikipedia.org/wiki/UNRWA

234. https://en.wikipedia.org/wiki/UNRWA

demonstrated the complexity of the problem and the geopolitical interests at play. While there was international recognition of the humanitarian crisis and some efforts to provide aid to displaced Palestinians, there was insufficient political will to take decisive action against the displacement and alleged ethnic cleansing.

The Arab nations took action by contingents of four of the seven countries of the Arab League at that time, Egypt, Iraq, Transjordan, and Syria, invaded the former British Mandate of Palestine, and fought the Israelis. They were supported by the Arab Liberation Army and a corps of volunteers from Saudi Arabia, Lebanon, and Yemen. The Arab armies launched a simultaneous offensive on all fronts: Egyptian forces invaded from the south, Jordanian and Iraqi forces from the east, and Syrian troops invaded from the north.

The U.N. declared a truce on May 29 in the war which began on June 11 and lasted 28 days. The ceasefire was overseen by U.N. mediator Folke Bernadotte and a team of U.N. Observers and army officers from Belgium, the United States, Sweden, and France.

An arms embargo was declared with the intention that neither side would make gains from the truce. Neither side respected the truce; both found ways around the restrictions. Both the Israelis and the Arabs used this time to improve their positions, a direct violation of the terms of the ceasefire.

Weapons were often disguised as regular cargo and transported to Palestine under cover of darkness. In addition to smuggling, the Jewish community established clandestine workshops for the production of arms and ammunition. These workshops, hidden in kibbutzim and beneath city streets, played a crucial role in expanding the Jewish weapons stockpile.

International Support The embargo was further undermined by both sides' support from sympathetic nations. Czechoslovakia, in defiance of the blockade, sold large quantities of arms to the Jewish forces.

This operation, known as **Operation**[235]**Balak**[236],[237] provided Israel with significant firepower, including rifles, machine guns, and even aircraft. On the Arab side, neighboring countries like Egypt, Jordan, and Syria provided material support, further fueling the conflict. Embargo enforcement needed to be more consistent and often more robust, further contributing to its failure. The British authorities tasked with overseeing the embargo were stretched thin and usually needed help to effectively police Palestine's vast coastline and borders. The Arab nations violated the truce by adding reinforcements from new units in Saudi Arabia, Yemen, and Morocco.

Israel continued to train men and women in the military and increased the number to 65,000 active service.

The remaining British forces released from confinement in Cyprus the illegal immigrants, many of whom then returned to Palestine and were added to the military forces.

Field Commander Fawzi AL-Qawugji established a headquarters with former British soldiers and police who hated Jews and wanted to fight them. There were many former British soldiers that defections from his officers, many of whom, like General John Bagot, joined the Jordanian Army.(55)

In the city of Safed, 12,000 people fled across the border into Syria, expecting military support to come from the neighboring Arab nations, but this took weeks to happen, and the properties and homes were taken by the Jews.(56) The IDF and the Haganah took control of the region and prevented the return of the Arabs to their homes. Palestinian refugee camps were established in Syria, where refugees lived in precarious conditions, often dependent on international aid for basic necessities.

---

235. https://en.wikipedia.org/wiki/Operation_Balak

236. https://en.wikipedia.org/wiki/Operation_Balak

237. https://en.wikipedia.org/wiki/Operation_Balak

Lebanon also received a significant influx of Palestinian refugees following the establishment of Israel. Palestinian refugees settled in camps across Lebanon, such as Ain al-Hilweh and Burj al-Barajneh. But by the end of the second truce, the British had almost entirely left Palestine, and Israel's IDF had completed the forced evacuation of the more than 700,000 Palestinians from the country.

The efforts to use the U.N. for peaceful diplomacy in the country became more complex, and the violence against Arab Palestinians by the Israeli government continued

Thomas Campbell Wasson, The Consul General for the United States in Jerusalem and a member of the Truce Commission in Palestine was given the task to maintain the Truce by working with both Arab and Jewish leaders to protect Jerusalem which was a neutral site.

He attempted to establish order in Jerusalem once the British Mandate ended on May 15, 1948. On May 22, Wasson attempted to stop the shelling of the Hadassah Hospital and Hebrew University on Mount Scopus. This was being done by the Arab Legion, but the Legion's leaders complained that the Jews were using it as a base to attack Jerusalem.

The Arab leader required that the Jews surrender and that the Doctors and nurses would also come out and surrender, and they would be turned over to the Red Cross. Wasson was shot and assassinated while returning to the U.S. Consulate from a meeting of the U.N. Truce Commission at the French Consulate in Jerusalem. The Jews were suspected because of the tension between the Jews and Arabs, but many claimed he was killed by Arabs.

Thomas Wasson was aware of the Hadassah convoy massacre that took place on April 13, 1948, when a convoy, escorted by Haganah militia, bringing medical and military supplies and personnel to Hadassah Hospital on Mount Scopus, Jerusalem, was ambushed by Arab forces. Seventy-eight Jewish doctors, nurses, students, patients were killed.

The Jewish[238] Agency[239] claimed that the massacre was a gross violation of international humanitarian law and demanded action be taken against a breach of the Geneva Conventions.

Arabs,the attack on the Hadassah convoy was a retaliation for the Deir Yassin massacre on April 9 1948.

Chapter # 14

The U.N. Last Chance for Peace Folke Bernadotte:

The U.N. Last Chance for Peace: Folke Bernadotte, the United Nations mediator appointed in 1948, plans a partition plan allowing displaced Arabs to return home and receive compensation for their lost property.(55)The Jewish Agency and the Arab Nationalists rejected the Plan for an equal state for self-governing. The Arab Leaders have no plan to return Palestinians to their homes and do not support the Plan for a partition by the U.N.

As a trained envoy, Folke Bernadotte had faced the danger of working with hostile parties to negotiate with. He had worked with Field Marshal Hinreich Himmler to save people held in the Nazi death camps in Germany. Many of those that he saved were Jews held in the concentration camps. Bernadotte received several awards from Zionist groups after the war.

Bernadotte established a first truce after the war began on May 15 and the end of the British Mandate.

He also was aware of the expulsion of hundreds of thousands of Palestinians by the Zionist IDF forces. His Plan was intended to allow them to return to their homes and land once an end to the war was reached. But it was clear that Israel planned on blocking any attempt for Palestinians to return to their land.

Arab leaders from Palestine had no plan on how to return the people except that they believed that the leaders of the Arab nations at war in the surrounding countries would support the Palestinians, force out

---

238. https://en.wikipedia.org/wiki/Jewish_Agency

239. https://en.wikipedia.org/wiki/Jewish_Agency

the Jews, and return their lands. The Arab nationalists believed that the best way to advance Palestinian interests was to operate within whichever regime was in power. They criticized the Arab Higher Committee's performance during the 1948 [240]Arab[241]-[242]Israeli[243]War[244] as being unaware and ineffective at best and ambivalent at worst to the needs of the Palestinian Arab population.

Folke Bernadotte believed that the zones he created if supported by the U.N., could support two nations with Jerusalem as a protected region by the U.N.

The Arab leaders mistakenly believed that they would be able to combine their forces, retake the region, and force out the Jews based on the use of a unified force.

Egypt, in the Plan, would attack Gaza from the south, Syria, and Transjordan with support from Saudi Arabia and Lebanon.

But Israel countered this with Israeli forces launching a simultaneous offensive on all three fronts: Dani, Dekel, and Kedem.

The battles lasted until a second truce was declared on July 18, lasting only 10 days. Egypt had captured Gaza and was moving north toward Tel Avi, while the forces from Iran attacked from the east.

Folke Bernadotte and the U.N., by September, believed this was the last chance to stop the war and allow for the safe return of the depopulated Palestinian people.

The Jewish Agency and the Arab League rejected the Partition plan before attempting to meet with them to discuss the changes.

The Zionist revisionist terrorist planned to prevent the U.N. Partition plan. The members of the Stern gang made the decision to assassinate

---

240. https://en.wikipedia.org/wiki/1948_Arab-Israeli_War

241. https://en.wikipedia.org/wiki/1948_Arab-Israeli_War

242. https://en.wikipedia.org/wiki/1948_Arab-Israeli_War

243. https://en.wikipedia.org/wiki/1948_Arab-Israeli_War

244. https://en.wikipedia.org/wiki/1948_Arab-Israeli_War

Bernadotte without the approval of the Yishiva or the Jewish agency. Bernadotte's partition plan was seen as a threat by the Zionists, especially his proposal that parts of the Negev desert be surrendered. On September 17, 1948, Count Folke Bernadotte, a United Nations Mediator for Palestine, was murdered in Jerusalem by a Zionist terrorist, the "Stern gang" Lehi.

T

The assassination of Swedish diplomat Folke Bernadotte in 1948 marked a critical juncture in the Arab-Israeli conflict.

As a United Nations mediator, Bernadotte had been tasked with brokering a peace deal between the Jewish and Arab communities in Palestine. His proposed partition plan aimed to create more viable territories for both Jews and Arabs and internationalize Jerusalem due to its religious and cultural significance. However, the rejection of his Plan by both parties and his subsequent assassination effectively closed the window of opportunity for a two-state solution that could have allowed Jews and Arabs to coexist peacefully in Palestine.

Bernadotte's partition plan was seen as a threat by the Zionists, especially his proposal that parts of the Negev desert be surrendered, which threatened their territorial gains and aspirations. The Arabs, on the other hand, rejected the Plan outright because it implicitly recognized the existence of Israel, something they were unwilling to accept. They perceived the creation of Israel as an imposition on the native Palestinian population. They insisted on the right of return for all Palestinian refugees who had been displaced during the war. The assassination of Bernadotte, by members of the Zionist paramilitary group Lehi, was a clear indication of the unwillingness of hardline segments within the Zionist movement to compromise on their territorial ambitions.

It also highlighted the volatility and danger mediators faced when brokering a peace deal in such a heated and complex conflict. On the other hand, the Arab nations' refusal to accept any plan that included the recognition of Israel demonstrated their uncompromising stance. Despite the displacement of Palestinian Arabs and the ongoing conflict, they remained staunch in their opposition to a Jewish state. In the aftermath of Bernadotte's death, no further substantial attempts were made to implement a two-state solution.

The conflict escalated into a full-blown war, leading to further displacement of Palestinians and solidifying the divisions between Jews and Arabs. The chance for a peaceful coexistence, as envisaged by Bernadotte, seemed to have been lost. The uncompromising positions adopted by both sides, coupled with the escalating violence, made a peaceful resolution increasingly unattainable.

The assassination of Bernadotte sent shockwaves around the world. It was a stark reminder of the volatility and danger surrounding attempts to broker peace in such a heated and complex conflict. The international community reacted with shock and condemnation. His death effectively closed the window of opportunity for a two-state solution, a solution that could potentially have allowed Jews and Arabs to coexist peacefully in Palestine.

The U.N. condemned Israel for the murder, and this ended all efforts for a partition plan between the Arab Nationalists and Israel. The Zionist leaders in Israel never condemned the assignation by Lehi. The assassination was a clear indication of the uncompromising stance of hardline segments within the Zionist movement. The U.S. government did not question the murder or withdraw the support for Israel.

In Israel, the reaction to Bernadotte's murder was one of shock and condemnation. The Israeli government quickly distanced itself from the actions of the Lehi, condemning the assassination and pledging to bring the perpetrators to justice. However, no members of the Lehi were ever prosecuted for Bernadotte's assassination, a fact that has remained a source of controversy.

The legacy of Bernadotte's failed peace initiative is a poignant reminder of the missed opportunities for peace in the decades-long Israeli-Palestinian conflict.

Britain protested the actions of the U.S. support of Israel and supplied Transjordan with weapons. U.S. President Truman supported Israel, and the U.S. provided supplies to aid to continue the fight against the Arab forces. Transjordan and Egypt received the majority of support from Britain for the war. The war began with the end of the British Mandate for Palestine and the subsequent declaration of independence by Israel on May 14, 1948. The Arab forces of Egypt, Transjordan, Syria, and Lebanon crossed the border into Israel, planning to force the Zionists out of Palestine.

The relationship between the Israeli Defense Forces (IDF) and the paramilitary groups Irgun (Irgun Tsvai-Leumi) and Lehi (Stern Gang) was complex. It evolved throughout the 1948 Arab-Israeli War and its aftermath. The dynamic between these entities was characterized by cooperation and conflict, reflecting the broader complexities and tensions within the Zionist movement.

During the 1948 war, the IDF and Irgun/Lehi forces coordinated and collaborated. This was particularly evident in joint military operations aimed at securing territory and countering the forces of neighboring Arab states.

In these instances, the common goal of establishing and defending a Jewish state overshadowed the ideological differences and rivalries between these groups. The shared mission must still erase the differences between the IDF and these paramilitary groups. The Irgun and Lehi were known for their more radical stance and willingness to use violence in pursuit of their objectives, which often put them at odds with the more mainstream elements of the Zionist movement, including those who led the IDF. The establishment of the State of Israel in May 1948 marked the beginning of a new phase in the relationship between the IDF and the Irgun and Lehi. The newly formed Israeli government sought to consolidate military command and control under the IDF,

This integration process was challenging. Many members of the Irgun and Lehi were deeply committed to their respective organizations and ideologies, which led to resistance and tensions. However, over time, many former members of these groups joined the IDF and continued to serve in various capacities. The integration of the Irgun and Lehi into the IDF marked the end of their existence as independent paramilitary groups.

However, these groups' legacy and their relationship with the IDF continued to influence Israeli politics and society in the following years.

During the 1948 war, the IDF and Irgun/Lehi forces coordinated and collaborated. This was particularly evident in joint military operations aimed at securing territory and countering the forces of neighboring Arab states.

The disbandment of Irgun and Lehi, two paramilitary groups that played a crucial role in the civil war against the Arabs, the British Mandate, the "Nakba," and the war in 1948, marked a significant turning point in the history of the State of Israel.

The newly formed Israeli government, led by David Ben-Gurion, sought to consolidate all military forces under the control of the Israel Defense Forces (IDF). This move aimed to create a unified, state-controlled military and to curtail the influence of radical paramilitary groups like Irgun and Lehi.

The integration process was fraught with challenges. Many members of Irgun and Lehi resisted the dissolution of their organizations and the loss of their independent command. This resistance culminated in the "Altalena Affair," a violent confrontation between the IDF and Irgun over a disputed arms shipment.

The incident, which resulted in several deaths, highlighted the deep-seated tensions within the Zionist movement and marked a turning point in the process of consolidating Israel's military forces. By the end of 1948, Irgun and Lehi had formally disbanded, and most of their members had integrated into the IDF. However, the legacies of these groups lived on. Many former members went on to have influential roles in Israeli politics and society, carrying their ideologies and experiences into their new roles. The disbandment of Irgun and Lehi and their integration into the IDF was pivotal in establishing the State of Israel. It marked the end of a period of fragmented and often radical Zionist militancy and the beginning of a unified, state-controlled military.

Chapter #15

The Armistice of 1949 between Israel and the Arab States at war. The armistice of 1949 between Israel and the Arab nations of Egypt, Syria, Lebanon, Saudi Arabia, and Yemen marked the end of the 1948 Arab-Israeli War, also known as the War of Independence in Israel.

The war and its resulting armistice significantly shaped the geopolitical landscape of the Middle East, with a series of decisive battles playing a critical role in determining its outcome.

The major battles begin between Israel and the Arab forces from all of the surrounding borders of Israel. The earliest and most significant war confrontation was the Battle of Latrun in May 1948. Israeli forces failed to capture the Latrun area, which was held by the Jordanian Arab Legion. This failure resulted in Jerusalem being cut off from the rest of Israel, and it remained a divided city until 1967.

Despite numerous attempts, Israeli forces failed to capture the Latrun area, which was held by the Jordanian Arab Legion. This failure cut Jerusalem off from the rest of Israel, . The Israeli Defense Forces (IDF) were more successful in the south. In Operation Yoav, launched in October 1948, the IDF broke the Egyptian blockade of the Negev desert.

This operation opened the way for further Israeli advances in the south, including Operation Horev in December 1948, which pushed Egyptian forces out of the Negev and to the borders of the Sinai Peninsula. In the north, the IDF launched Operation Hiram in October 1948, aiming to push back Lebanese, Syrian, and Palestinian irregular forces.

The operation was largely successful, capturing the upper Galilee region and securing the Lebanese border.

The armistice agreements in 1949 were negotiated separately with each of the involved Arab states.

The agreements demarcated the armistice lines, also known as the[245] Green[246] Line[247],[248] intended to serve as a temporary border until a permanent peace agreement could be reached.(57)

However, no such agreement was reached, and the Green Line ultimately became the de facto border of the State of Israel. The 1948 Arab-Israeli War was characterized by multiple battles that determined the outcome of the conflict and shaped the borders of the newly established State of Israel. The armistice of 1949 marked the end of the outright war, but a precarious peace set the stage for further regional conflicts.

The armistice began in 1949, with Moshe Dayan representing Israel and Ralph Bunche representing the U.N.

The negotiations resulted in the establishment of the Green Line, a ceasefire line marking Israel's territorial gains.

The Green Line became the de facto border, separating Israel from the West Bank, Gaza Strip, and Golan Heights.

The armistice agreements demarcated the armistice lines with each involved Arab state.

---

245. https://en.wikipedia.org/wiki/Green_Line_(Israel)

246. https://en.wikipedia.org/wiki/Green_Line_(Israel)

247. https://en.wikipedia.org/wiki/Green_Line_(Israel)

248. https://en.wikipedia.org/wiki/Green_Line_(Israel)

Moshe Dayan, a prominent Israeli military leader, was Israel's primary representative in the negotiations with the United Nations (U.N.). Dayan was well-known for his pragmatism and strategic acumen, which were instrumental in navigating the intricacies of the ceasefire talks. Despite the tense atmosphere and high stakes, Dayan effectively presented the Israeli perspective and ensured the inclusion of critical Israeli demands in the final agreement.(58) On the other side of the negotiation table was Ralph[249]Bunche[250], an American diplomat serving as the United Nations representative. Bunche was a seasoned diplomat known for his mediation skills and deep understanding of international conflicts. He had been actively involved in the Palestine issue even before the outbreak of the war, having assisted

Bunche's diplomatic skills were crucial in bridging the gap between the conflicting parties and reaching a mutually agreeable solution. His ability to maintain an impartial position while effectively mediating between the parties was critical in establishing trust and ensuring the success of the negotiations. The negotiations were marked by intensive meetings, during which various issues were discussed, ranging from ceasefire lines to the return of displaced persons. The most significant outcome of these negotiations was the establishment of the Green Line, which was essentially a ceasefire line marking the territorial gains made by Israel during the war. The Green Line, so named because it was drawn in green ink on the map used during the negotiations, became the de facto border of Israel, separating it from the West Bank, Gaza Strip, and Golan Heights.

Despite its temporary nature, the Green Line became a permanent feature of the region.

It was intended to serve only as a ceasefire line, not a final border, with the understanding that a comprehensive peace agreement would

---

249. https://en.wikipedia.org/wiki/Ralph_Bunche

250. https://en.wikipedia.org/wiki/Ralph_Bunche

eventually be negotiated. However, in the absence of a final settlement, the Green Line has become the internationally recognized border of Israel, serving as the basis for future peace proposals. The negotiations between Moshe Dayan and Ralph Bunche leading to the creation of the Green Line were a defining moment in the history of the Israeli-Palestinian conflict. The Green Line, a product of these negotiations, is a focal point in ongoing discussions about resolving the dispute. These armistice lines roughly corresponded to the boundaries of the territories held by each side at the end of the 1948 war, with minor adjustments in some areas. The armistice agreements did not address the underlying issues of Palestinian displacement and the status of Palestinian refugees.

Hundreds of thousands of Palestinians had been displaced from their homes during the 1948 war, leading to the creation of a large refugee population. Following the 1948 Arab-Israeli War, Israel took several actions to prevent the return of the Palestinian people who had been displaced during the conflict. These actions were driven by various security concerns, demographic considerations, and political motives.

Israel's Policies to Control Refugees Post-Armistice

- Israel enacted laws and regulations to bar the return of Palestinian refugees.

- The 1950 Law of Return granted Jews worldwide the right to immigrate to Israel and gain citizenship.

- The[251] Absentees[252'] [253]Property[254]Law[255]of[256] 1950[257] allowed Israel to take control of lands and properties left behind by displaced Palestinians.

One of the main strategies adopted by Israel was the enactment of laws and regulations that effectively barred the return of Palestinian refugees. The 1950 Law of Return granted Jews worldwide the right to immigrate to Israel and gain citizenship. Still, no equivalent provision was made for Palestinians who had fled or been expelled during the war.

The Absentees' Property Law of 1950 also allowed Israel to take control of lands and properties left behind by Palestinians who had been displaced, further complicating the prospects of return.

On the ground, Israel undertook measures to alter the physical landscape of the areas from which Palestinians had been displaced. Many Palestinian villages were demolished, and new Jewish settlements were built in their place. This not only made it physically impossible for many Palestinians to return to their original homes but also aimed to solidify Jewish presence and control over these areas. At the international level, Israel opposed initiatives aimed at facilitating the return of Palestinian refugees.

Israel's Rejection of U.N. Resolution 194

Israel rejected U.N. General Assembly Resolution 194, passed in December 1948, which affirmed the right of Palestinian refugees to return home or receive compensation.

---

251. https://en.wikipedia.org/wiki/Israeli_land_and_property_laws

252. https://en.wikipedia.org/wiki/Israeli_land_and_property_laws

253. https://en.wikipedia.org/wiki/Israeli_land_and_property_laws

254. https://en.wikipedia.org/wiki/Israeli_land_and_property_laws

255. https://en.wikipedia.org/wiki/Israeli_land_and_property_laws

256. https://en.wikipedia.org/wiki/Israeli_land_and_property_laws

257. https://en.wikipedia.org/wiki/Israeli_land_and_property_laws

The armistice lines resulted in the division of historic Palestine, with the West Bank and Gaza Strip under separate control.(59)
Israel rejected the United Nations General Assembly Resolution 194, passed in December 1948, which affirmed the right of Palestinian refugees to return to their homes or to receive compensation for their losses if they chose not to return.
The Result of the Armistice Lines

- Division of Historic Palestine

  o The West Bank came under Jordanian control.

  o The Gaza Strip came under Egyptian control.

- Territorial Control by Israel

  o Israel retained control over most of the territory allocated to it by the U.N. Partition Plan of 1947.

Israel argued that the return of Palestinian refugees would upset the demographic balance of the newly established Jewish state and pose a threat to its security. Israel's stance on the Palestinian right of return has remained essentially unchanged over the decades despite ongoing peace negotiations and international pressure. The issue of Palestinian refugees continues to be one of the most contentious aspects of the Israeli-Palestinian conflict, with the right of return being a key demand of Palestinians.
Following the 1948 war, Israel implemented a series of measures designed to prevent the return of displaced Palestinians. These actions, underpinned by legal, physical, and political strategies, have significantly shaped the course of the Israeli-Palestinian conflict and continue to impact the prospects for its resolution. The armistice lines resulted in the division of historic Palestine, with the West Bank and Gaza Strip coming under Jordanian and Egyptian control,

respectively. Israel retained control over most of the territory allocated to it by the U.N. Partition Plan of 1947(60)

Impact on Modern Israeli-Palestinian Relations

The history of Zionist terrorism and the violent birth of the Palestinian state have cemented a legacy of mistrust, fear, and animosity. These historical episodes are not mere relics of the past but active elements shaping the political, social, and psychological landscapes of Israelis and Palestinians.

Conclusion

The creation of the state of Israel was deeply intertwined with the use of militant tactics and terrorism, a legacy that continues to shape the region today. From 1917 to 1949, Zionist groups like Irgun, Lehi, and Haganah engaged in violent resistance against British authorities and Palestinian Arabs. These groups, through bombings, assassinations, and military operations, hastened the end of British control and secured vital territories for the emerging Jewish state. While their actions contributed to the establishment of Israel, they also displaced many Palestinians, laying the groundwork for a conflict that endures to this day.

The foundation of Israel, built in part on campaigns of militancy, has had lasting effects on the Israeli-Palestinian conflict. The tactics used by these groups, and their broader consequences, continue to influence the policies, attitudes, and narratives in the region. Today, the legacy of violence and resistance that marked Israel's early formation persists, creating an ongoing cycle of conflict and retaliation that complicates efforts toward lasting peace. The roots of modern tensions are firmly embedded in the historical events that shaped Israel's creation, with their echoes still felt in contemporary Israeli and Palestinian society.

The challenges stemming from the Sykes-Picot Agreement of 1916, which drew arbitrary borders across the Middle East without consideration for the region's complex demographic realities, continue to shape the Israeli-Palestinian conflict in 2024. Despite numerous attempts by the international community, including the U.N. Partition Plan of 1947 and the more recent peace initiatives proposed by U.S. Presidents, the fundamental issues remain unresolved.

U.S. presidents, from President Bush to President Obama, have recognized Israel as a critical ally in the Middle East, prioritizing its security and sovereignty in their diplomatic efforts. For decades, U.S. foreign policy has been shaped by the notion that a stable and secure Israel is essential for regional stability. However, the prioritization of Israel as an indispensable strategic partner has often complicated efforts to broker a balanced solution to the Israeli-Palestinian conflict. While the two-state solution has been championed as the most viable path to peace, it has repeatedly failed to address the deeply entrenched historical and territorial grievances on both sides.

The Sykes-Picot Agreement laid the groundwork for these ongoing tensions by carving up the region without the consent of the local populations, and its legacy continues to affect Jews and Arabs alike. The unresolved issues of sovereignty, identity, and territorial claims that arose from this colonial-era arrangement have been exacerbated by modern geopolitical interests. As successive U.S. administrations have reinforced Israel's strategic importance, the broader context of Palestinian dispossession and statehood has often been sidelined, perpetuating the conflict.

In 2024, the lines drawn in 1917 still echo, as the core issues of land, identity, and justice remain unresolved. Until both Israeli and Palestinian narratives are reconciled and the historical grievances addressed, any peace initiative, no matter how well-intentioned will struggle to bring about lasting peace. The failure of previous peace efforts underscores that only a solution which genuinely accounts for both sides' aspirations—beyond geopolitical alliances—can hope to break the century-long impasse.

Don't miss out!

Visit the website below and you can sign up to receive emails whenever rajib christian publishes a new book. There's no charge and no obligation.

https://books2read.com/r/B-A-ARDMC-XZRDF

BOOKS2READ

Connecting independent readers to independent writers.

About the Author

Rajib Christian is an investigative journalist and truth-seeker with a passion for uncovering the stories most people don't want to talk about. Whether it's exposing hidden histories or confronting today's systemic injustices, Rajib dives into the tough topics that challenge the status quo and demand accountability.In Rajib's latest book, How Jewish Terrorists Created the State of Israel, they take readers on a deep dive into one of history's most controversial chapters. This groundbreaking exposé unpacks the violent and often-overlooked tactics that shaped the founding of Israel. For Rajib, this book isn't just about history—it's a personal mission to shed light on the forces of power, violence, and oppression that still resonate today.Rajib's passion for justice extends far beyond the pages of their latest book. They've also written extensively about social issues, including the exploitation of Black women in the music industry. Their powerful article, "R. Kelly, Chris Brown, and Russell Simmons: A Portrait of the Music Industry and the Victimization of Black Women," opened critical conversations about the intersection of fame, abuse, and silence.When not writing, Rajib is a relentless researcher, a listener to untold stories, and a believer in the power of truth to spark change. Whether digging into archives or amplifying the voices of the silenced, Rajib Christian brings curiosity, courage, and a deep commitment to justice to everything they do. Connect with Rajib on [website or social media links] and discover their latest work, available now.

Read more at https://amazon.com/author/booksbyrajib3352.

About the Publisher